It'll Be Okay In The Morning

A Life Story

Brian Cosacchi

Copyright © 2011 Brian Cosacchi
All rights reserved.

ISBN: 1-4611-3407-2
ISBN-13: 9781461134077

Contents

	Preface ix
	Prologue xiii
1.	Roots 1
	The Italians.. 2
	The Irish 4
2.	An Unlikely Couple 7
3.	Harrison 11
4.	Bruce 17
5.	The Spencer Pharmacy 19
6.	#3 Second Street—Home 23
7.	Matches 29
8.	Roseanne Quinn 31
9.	My First Cigar 33
10.	Sheila 37
11.	Winter 41
12.	Radio 45
13.	TV 47
14.	The Big Game 49
15.	Being Catholic 53
16.	Altar Boys 55
17.	The Water Rats of Oakland Beach 59
18.	Boy Scouts, Camp Siwanoy and The Order of the Arrow 63
19.	Piano Lessons 69
20.	Dr. Finelli 73
21.	Elementary School 79
22.	Last Years of Elementary School—6th Grade 83
23.	Aunt Angelina's 87
24.	Darkness: The Attic and the Cellar 91
25.	Hide and Go Seek 95

26.	On to High School	101
27.	The Kiss	105
28.	Notre Dame	111
29.	Mrs. Helen Mulrey	115
30.	The Military	121
31.	Getting Married	133
32.	Leaving the Military Womb—On Our Own	139
33.	Kankakee, Illinois	145
34.	Adjusting to Dog (Food) Days	151
35.	Les' Dream—A Nightmare	155
36.	Our First Home	163
37.	The Job	167
38.	The Clown Car	169
39.	Tara	171
40.	Karin—Our Third Child—Thy Will Be Done	175
41.	Captains (not so) Courageous	179
42.	Finally, A Second Child	185
43.	Getting On With Life	191
44.	Going Over The Top	197
45.	Sailing on Lake Candlewood	201
46.	A Skating Adventure with Tara	205
47.	Kent/Saint Howard of Schneider	211
48.	A Trip To Europe	215
49.	Capitulation	225
50.	John O'Hara	229
51.	A Decisive Year—Intervention	233
52.	Good Bye John	239
53.	Charleston—Meet Lisa	241
54.	A Difficult Retirement	243
55.	A Christmas To Remember	247
56.	The Inevitable	251
57.	—And then there were Two	255
58.	Maybe Just A Bad Dream	261
59.	The House That 'Crack" Built 2006—2007	265
60.	Searching for Another Bottom	269

61.	We Needed An Attorney	275
62.	Continuing Our New Adventure!	283
63.	Lisa's Final Collapse—For Now	287
64.	Intermission	291

Preface

I've been retired for 13 years—one of the very lucky ones who had enough guff from the corporate sideshow—danced the "career" for 25 years, and had sense not to entirely trust the corporate clowns in their Savile Row suits and accumulated enough to be able to break out into a kinder, gentler life. So, I've had time to play music and games and watch the world stagger along. It's been fun!

Now, as my sweet-faced wife and I slip into the golden twilight years, God has decided to saddle us with a couple of young kids—grandchildren thrust upon us by The Almighty via parents who struggle with life.

It's been almost three years since the kids have come to live with us. We have almost completely accepted their intrusion into our comfortable, happy retired life. They are both a blessing and an obligation—something to finish before we go. And while Les and I are far from perfect as second-time-around parents, the kids are doing okay, all things considered. Some might think that a miracle considering they were brought into this world by a drug addicted mom who suffers from bipolar disorder and/or borderline personality and seems to enjoy it. She won't admit it and would rather wallow in it at the expense of her kids than get any sustained help. For most people, to meet her is a neutral experience. But to know her is to become afflicted.

And the kids' dad? Well, he's a recovering addict. He's been recovering on and off for about twenty years. We hope and pray and timidly believe he's got it right this time. He's had a tough life, born legally blind, picked on as a kid. Then lots of bad decisions! Most of them in recent years revolving around his (hopefully now divorced) wife, Lisa. Chris has bounced back and forth, to and from Medusa, her waist-long tresses captivating and, like Medusa, turning him into "stoned."

I just became a septuagenarian. My sweet-faced wife is a few years younger. We continue on this highway of life, replete with detours, potholes, washouts, and occasional stretches of smooth, comfortable riding and new adventures every time we stop.

But this road will end long, long before we see as many miles as we have already traveled. Every septuagenarian thinks about death—the end of the road. There is sober reflection about time spent and time remaining. There is consideration of one's life and whether one's aspirations have been met. Everyone's got aspirations even if they don't know it until they think about it as death arrives. Sometimes it's too late.

For some it's, "Did I do enough? Will this world be a better place because I was here? Did I make a difference? Will I merit heaven? Will I be remembered?" Maybe most of all, "Will I be remembered?"

I think I've tried to help here and there—basically a good enough person now being tested. But when I look at the world as it is now, I shake this old bald head in despair. I look at my innocent grandchildren and almost wish I could take them with me when I go because I know, wherever I go will be easier than what they will likely face on this earth in their lifetime.

I pray they can dig around in the pages of this life's moraine and turn up some useful nuggets. Maybe that's the best I can offer.

I will also confess a record of my life is something I'd like to leave behind; something better than a headstone—maybe more enduring.

I'd like to believe I'll be remembered because I can't completely shake lingering doubts about the existence of a "hereafter." I am sacrilegiously hedging my bet. This book is a feeble attempt at achieving some cheap immortality because, after we pass, we continue to live as long as we are remembered. For most of us that's not very long. New memories grow on old ones like new grass on top of old dead clippings. I'm hoping this book will force the new grass and weeds to grow around it.

So, here is the story of Brian Cosacchi growing up and old and some of the fun, adventures problems and mistakes I've made.

Finally, I dedicate this book to my mom and dad who rest peacefully in St. Mogues Cemetery in County Cavan, Ireland. (Dad swore that's where mom wanted to be buried after she died so we shipped her over. When Dad passed he wanted to lie with her one more time—forever. So we shipped him over too. The folks at St. Mogues in Bawnboy had to squeeze a few plots together to make room for both Mom and Dad, but you can be sure these are the only two 'Cosacchi' graves in all of Ireland.)

Peter and Kathleen weren't particularly good parents, what with the alcohol and a lot of yelling and some hitting, but they may have loved each other, and they tried hard. So, if anyone does read any of this, Mom and Dad get much of the credit for the good and the bad.

Prologue

I hadn't seen her in three years. Not since they moved to Seattle out of desperation. They gave up Harrison, New York, after fifty years. Mom's alcoholism contributed to her diabetes and Parkinson's and a host of aches and pains. Dad tried to take care of her. He even converted her from booze to drugs thinking, as a pharmacist, he could better manage the dosage and the end result. But time was passing them by, and over the past fifteen years Mom, now 70 plus, had progressively become an invalid. So they moved to Seattle to be with my brother, Bruce. He was single and had plenty of room. I don't think he knew what he was getting into, and I wasn't going to tell him. I couldn't wait for them to leave. It was his turn.

Except for a couple of one- or two-day trips Bruce hadn't been back to Harrison in years. He hadn't had to live with the tiresome dysfunction that was Mom and Dad. I worked in White Plains then, only 8 miles or so from their Harrison home, and it was expected that I stop by for lunch each week. I didn't come close to meeting expectations. The disappointed telephone calls made me roll my eyes in frustration, but I still felt the guilt zingers. "Where were you today? We thought you'd be down to see your mother. She always looks forward to your visits. You cheer her up."

"How is she today?"

"Not so well. We know you must be busy so I'll let you go. Maybe you can come by sometime when you're not so busy—spend a few minutes with your mother. We'll be here, you know. No need to call ahead. She misses you."

Bruce didn't recall the dark days of living in the little stucco house on Second Street. He was a couple of years older than I and missed some of it. My sister Sheila caught the brunt, having to live through a lot of it alone when both Bruce and I went off to Notre Dame and left her at their mercy. She deserves a new life—a "do over.'

But now they lived out there in Seattle with Bruce, and he was learning and remembering how difficult it was trying to play referee and feel the guilt pile up as one parent played him against the other. Eventually Dad was no longer able to manage. And when he had done all he could to the point of exhaustion and dropped down on his 75-year-old knees on the kitchen floor and cried and begged his favored son for help, Bruce did what he could. Mom would rather have died than go to a nursing home.

With absolute recalcitrance she entered the home—one of the best in the Seattle area. But, in fairness I guess, like anyone who is incarcerated against his or her wishes and knows it is the last step before death, she did her best to get even. And Mom was good at it.

I wrangled a business trip to Seattle to fulfill my obligation—to say good-bye to the mother I can't recall ever having loved.

I arrived at the nursing home having planned to meet Dad and Bruce there. Mom's new and last home was everyman's description of a nursing home: low, plain, sterile looking brick, small windows peeking out, anemic, untended shrubs that looked appropriate in their end-of-life environment.

Bruce and Dad had not arrived, but the receptionist suggested I go on down to the Activities Room where Mom was waiting. I tried to look grateful and anxious to see my mother, but in fact I was looking forward to getting it over with and getting away. They gave me simple directions. I hurried through the hallways, avoiding half dead people asleep or unconscious in their wheel chairs. The smell of urine and bleach burned, and I took short breaths. I hurried. The quicker you get there, the quicker you get out.

It had been three years since I had seen her, and when I arrived at the Activities Room, I peeked in, scanning to locate Mom. Maybe I could sneak up on her the way I used to as a kid and sing her a song or just say something funny. But I couldn't find her among the dozen or so dozing, distant, vacant faces. She was there somewhere.

An attendant approached and asked who I was looking for. "Kathleen Cosacchi," I said. "I'm supposed to meet my brother and father here, but the receptionist said I could come down and visit with my mother while I waited for them."

"Certainly," he replied politely. "There's your mom right over there." Pointing to a wheel chair with the pathetic, decrepit, lifeless-looking remains of what might have been a woman at some time long ago.

I don't know what I said. I thought, *No, it can't be! That's not my mother! It looks nothing like my mother. Surely I would recognize my own mother. Wouldn't I? Wouldn't I?* I'm sure I gasped, choked a little. *How could I go and talk to THAT? That's not my mother!* I was repulsed and felt guilty and disgusted with myself. *Get your ass over there and give it a hug, you jerk. That's what's left of your mother. Put that other crap behind you for now. She's still your mother, and, God help her, she needs help—she needs you.*

I worked up a smile and put a spring in my step. I tentatively approached the old crone facing me now in her wheel chair. A blanket covered her legs. What was left of her hair, just a few gossamer wisps, hung like cobwebs from her scalp. She was expressionless except for an odd glint in her eyes. And I recognized that odd glint. This was indeed what was left of my mother. I smiled harder, "Hey Mom, it's Brigs! How're ya doin? Been a long time." No response, but the glint hardened. "What a great place," I lied.

"So, how are you, Mom?" No response. But the glint sent the message. I'd seen it often over the years. It was usually accompanied by a few words that expertly, purposely, thinly disguised disappointment and heaped on guilt and shame.

Without saying a word she told me: "You did this. You let them do this. I'm disappointed in you. You don't love your mother. I wish I were dead. I'll die here because of you."

"I'm glad you're here, Mom. Looks like you're well taken care of, and I know Dad wasn't able to take care of you any more. It's really the best thing. Don't you think?"

She turned her head away from me, cold, hard, hurtful silence. It was her way of fighting back, getting even, defending herself. I never understood it, but people who know me best tell me I do much the same when angry. Maybe it's better than cursing and yelling and hitting.

Mom always had a special way of withholding expressions of love or any positive warm human feeling. She was expert at disdain, disappointment and disapproval. I recall the Christmases Dad would try and buy her love with extravagant gifts, kneeling by her side like a loyal little terrier, tongue and tail wagging, "Oh boy, go ahead Dear, open it up, aw go ahead, oh boy, oh boy!" She methodically opened the gifts without expression; the mouton coat, the diamond Hamilton watch. Then the inevitable verdict—the off-handed, dismissive, patronizing, "Oh, that's nice, Dear" response. And, then without emotion—not even a second look, not even a "thank you" she placed it down beside her on the floor and looked away for another gift. I felt sorry for Dad on those Christmases. But he never did give up. That's the way life was growing up in our little house in Harrison, New York.

Chapter 1.
Roots

Over the past century or so we've become very diverse as a nation, diluting our roots into a multi cultural odd tasting stew in the great American melting pot. My grandchildren don't have much feeling for their Irish, English, Welsh, Czech, Italian heritage. But 100 years ago when Kathleen Devine and Peter Cosacchi met, ethnic and cultural differences were enormous walls to climb. People were bound by language, customs, traditions, and superstition to "stick with their own kind." Real differences among cultures kept people apart. And if individuals chose to ignore the "rules" it sometimes led to misunderstandings, disillusion and unhappiness. Part of the dismay that confounded our family came from that kind of misunderstanding.

My parents came from two different worlds in the way they looked at life, felt, and expressed feelings. On the Italian side, Dad's family was passionate and effusive; kissing and hugging and laughing and crying and yelling and loving each other. On the Irish side, Mom was dark, fatalistic, subdued, proud, restrained, subtle and withholding. I think my mother desperately wanted affection but didn't know how to ask for it or give it freely. Certainly there was more to the dysfunction that overwhelmed my parents than cultural differences, but whether genetic or learned, the fundamental differences between Kathleen and Peter created a festering breeding ground for depression and alienation.

The Italians

Il Cosacchi: The name means "Cossacks." Cossacks were fierce, marauding horsemen from the Steppe of Central Asia. They crisscrossed Eastern and Central Europe from the 14th through the 17th centuries and settled all over Eastern Europe. There is no record of them ever reaching Calabria, Sicily, or anywhere in Italy. So how "Il Cosacchi" ever got to Calabria and why they would ever want to stay in such an inhospitable place is a puzzlement.

Calabria has a beautiful and bountiful seacoast, but rocks and high cliffs make it hard to access. Over the centuries a constant stream of invaders sent most of the people into the hills to survive. The result is that Calabrese are a rich mixture of Greek and Roman, French and Spanish, and lots of other European tribes who traipsed across Italy's toe on the way to or from conquering someplace important. They bedded down there to rest after a hard decade or two of murder and pillage and left behind a little of their culture and a lot of their DNA.

I can't find too many Cosacchis left in Europe. I searched our name on the Internet and found one left in Calabria. He's a musician, Giuseppe Cosacchi. He plays authentic Calabrian music on a diatonic accordion with locals performing the vocals. (Not something you'd want to hear more than once, believe me!) But it's interesting to me because there is so much music bouncing around in the Cosacchi family. Maybe our branch of the Cossacks was in their military band. It's a mystery!

There is a Stephan Cosacchi born in 1903 in Budapest, Hungary. His father was born in Vienna. Stephan was a noted musicologist and composer, having studied under Liszt and Bartok. He wrote a few hundred classical pieces. There's even a square in the small German town of Franken-

It'll Be Okay In The Morning

thal named for a Stephan Cosacchi. I don't know if he has any connection to my family. I'd like to think so—more of that music connection.

My ancestors, the Cosacchis of Calabria, came through Ellis Island in the early 1900s along with millions of others from all over Europe to escape poverty.

The head of the family, my grandfather, Anthony Cosacchi, came with his mother, Catherine, and his three sisters, Florence, Minnie and Angelina. These three quintessential Italian aunts were the quiet family glue with gold tooth and a golden heart. Minnie and Angelina married and became D'Ambrosia and Santoro. Florence remained a happy spinster.

The Italian Cossacks initially settled in Bridgeport, Connecticut. Florence moved to Port Chester, New York, and took on a blue-collar production job at the local Life Savers plant. The rest of the family pooled their resources and bought a big house on Ellsworth Street in Rye, New York, in the 1920s.

That big house on Ellsworth Street was our place of congregation on major holidays as we grew up—Thanksgiving, Christmas and Easter—as well as weddings and funerals.

Anthony married Catherine Pertrosine. They had two sons, Joseph, and my dad, Peter. Catherine died shortly after Dad was born.

His father played the role of impresario, importing movies and acts from Italy. Unfortunately, that didn't work out very well, nor did any of the other dreams and schemes he ran after. Anthony lived and loved the fictional portrayal of himself on his theatre poster: Impresario Antonio Cosacchi, black cape and fedora pulled down over his forehead; mysterious, seductive, and a bon vivant. In reality, Grandpa was a failure who relied on the good will of the family for financial support and the raising of his two sons.

As a boy growing up I was aware of my grandfather's failure, and I asked my dad why he was still so tolerant and giving to his father. He told me "No matter what he does, he's still my father, and I will respect him." I thought, but didn't say, "Respect has to be earned."

The Italian side of the family was large and tight. For several, Italian was their first language. For Great Grandma it was her only language outside of her standard greeting: a pinch on the cheek while proclaiming, "Nice-a, nice-a." The Cosacchis were true to their culture, tradition and language.

But my dad was alone. He needed someone.

The Irish:
The countryside of Ireland is beautiful: lush green hills, sparkling lakes, babbling brooks and singing streams. But the melody plays over a passacaglia of poverty and deprivation, a legacy from centuries of bitter British occupation.

The Irish survived through 800 years of British brutality bordering on genocide. They endured the atrocities of Cromwell and lived through The Great Famine of the 18th century, used by the British to starve three fourths of the population. In 1729 Jonathan Swift satirically summarized the British attitude toward the Irish, "Irish children should become food, rather than eat food."

But the Irish endured. Their victory left them with extraordinary pride for having survived, extraordinary sadness

It'll Be Okay In The Morning

for having suffered, a fatalistic view of life for never having been able to look beyond tomorrow, hatred for their British oppressors and an unfortunate penchant for the drink, having had to dull the pain and sorrow for all those generations.

My mother, Kathleen, was a Devine, not a Divine. It's an ancient Celtic name that goes back to the Tirkennedy clan of County Fermanagh, an offshoot of the McGuires as far back as the third century. The Devines were bards and poets, keeping the history of Ireland alive in story and song.

Kathleen grew up in those sad rolling hills. With her parents John and Ellen, her two brothers, John and James, and her sister, Margaret, she lived in a medieval cottage with a dirt floor and sod roof. Her father scraped out a bit of a living farming in reluctant soil and dipping into the beautiful, stingy lake that never gave up quite enough. But the children all went to school and all claimed the silver tongue gift of the Irish.

In the mid 1920s a new depression descended on the world. People of Ireland were suffering again. To ease the burden Margaret came to the United States to seek her fortune, working as a maid for wealthy New York families. In 1930 at the age of 18, Kathleen also left home to join Margaret. She wouldn't return for more than 50 years. She wouldn't be there when her father died nor see her mother to her grave. Over the years she would recall her home and family with pride, nostalgically, wistfully recalling events from her past. Her Irish brogue would thicken as she recalled the bright times of her childhood. The dirt floors and the pain of the hard living became faint memories along with those of her mother and father, and the loch.

She was alone. She needed someone too.

Mom and Dad found each other like the Titanic and the iceberg.

Chapter 2.
An Unlikely Couple

Dad was a little man at about 5'6" and, in his younger years, weighed about 120 pounds. He had dark black hair and a rather long Italian nose. He wore thick glasses and had milky white skin. He was an Italian "geek"—very unmacho—and embarrassing to me as I was growing up. He wasn't a "man's man." He didn't know one end of a baseball bat from the other and threw a ball like a girl. He hadn't had any opportunity to play sports as a kid. As a teenager he was involved in a serious auto accident that sent him flying 100 feet through the windshield of the car, leaving him with a permanently injured back.

Sometimes he tried to shoot a basket or two with a few of the neighborhood boys. I held my breath and wandered off a bit, hoping it would end quickly. I didn't give him much credit for trying.

Dad graduated from Fordham University's School of Pharmacy—a significant achievement for the "orphaned" son of immigrant Italians!

After graduating he worked at Machia's Drug Store in Rye, and on weekends he worked as a waiter at Macri's Beer Garden at Playland Amusement Park. On one star-crossed weekend Kathleen Devine dropped by Macri's Beer Garden on a day off. She found both refreshment and Pete.

They began to try to scale the cultural barriers, seeing each other in secret, against the taboos of the day that kept cultural bloodlines pure. Dad's family suspected and began spying. They wanted to save him from himself. They were well intentioned, as they wanted to be sure he didn't mix with the wrong kind. Poor Irish immigrant girls were high on the wrong-kind list.

A confrontation was inevitable.

On summer days their love and passion brought them together in clandestine meetings. And on one of those days, as they met and embraced in front of Mal and Irving Steinberg's hamburger stand at Oakland Beach, the inevitable happened. Dad's three bloodhound aunts had tracked them down; three wicked witches bearing down on them. Mom and Dad saw them coming a quarter mile away, but there was nowhere to hide. The old ladies didn't slow their stride as they approached. They stopped inches from Kathleen's face and attacked, cawing and snipping, prancing like crows tormenting their prey. *"Tu non puttana bene! Stare lontano dal nostro ragazzo."* ("You no good whore. Leave our boy alone!")

Mom didn't understand the words, but the gestures and yelling essentially said, "You stink." She was frightened, desperate. She had no one except Pete. She believed she would at least always have him, and she had little choice but to hang on—stick it out. Maybe one day she could forgive the family. Maybe one day she would be accepted, and they could live happily as a family—maybe one day.

They were married above the muted objections of the Cosacchis and Santoros. The bride's side of the aisle was empty. No one from Ireland; no Devines or McGoverns or

It'll Be Okay In The Morning

Plunketts were there. Kathleen was still alone, but at least she was alone with Pete.

They began their life together in 1936. They settled in Harrison, New York, a small town sandwiched between Rye, Mamaroneck, and White Plains, about 30 minutes from Manhattan by train.

It was close enough to Machia's drug store in Rye for Pete to commute, close enough to family in Rye and Port Chester to keep in touch and share holidays and lives. But far enough away so that Kathleen wouldn't feel shunned, and the wounds might heal.

They found a small apartment in the Calvert Apartments, the tallest building in Harrison, rising six stories. It was built just across the railroad bridge from the village. The apartments were small, the hallways dark but clean. A potpourri of fragrances from a dozen different kitchens greeted you as you entered. And on a cold winter day the smells were enough to keep you warm. Harrison was a good place to begin.

Chapter 3.
Harrison

In 1695 the Siwanoy Indians granted John Harrison a boon. He could have as much land as he could ride his horse around in a single day. Harrison had some trouble riding in straight lines, what with rivers and other natural obstacles, so the 22 square miles that comprise Harrison's borders are very irregular. But in the 1940s the town was as "regular" and "four square" as it could be. Andy Hardy would have fit in comfortably, especially had he been Italian. It was a wonderful town to raise a family. Crime was virtually unheard of. Harrison was "Our Town."

It was a happy mixture of western European nationalities: Italian, Irish, Scottish, and German. A few Jewish families lived there, mostly up on the ritzy Sunny Ridge and Pleasant Ridge sections of town and on the Westchester Country Club grounds. We even had a Negro family or two. But the town was and still is unquestionably Italian and Catholic. People got along well, although some very old Italian families who lived across the tracks stayed to themselves. A few never learned to speak English.

The town's leader was a First Selectman, a part time job. The position was held for most of my growing up years by a local attorney named Al Sulla. Al held the position for years until the jealous husband of a woman he was representing in a divorce case broke into his office and bit off his nose. The ambulance crew was alert enough to scoop up the nose, and doctors were able to sew it back on. But Al had to take some time off to give his nose a rest, and he gave up the position. His nose survived although the stitches were very noticeable, and it always looked as though it was about to fall off again. I don't recall if the woman's divorce went through.

Looking back now, Harrison was a pleasant dream; soft clouds, open meadows, deep dark woodlands, a convivial village, and comfortable people to be with. These were quieter, gentler times.

There were a couple of small farms on the west side of town. The Lawrence Brothers who lived about two miles away on West Street had an egg farm and raised rabbits. I don't think either of them was married. They delivered their eggs directly to our home in a very old black Ford truck. It could have been a Model T. They looked like twins, and they even smelled alike, like musty old wet clothes mixed with chicken feathers and tobacco. They chewed tobacco, and it leaked a little from the corners of their mouths and dribbled and dried on the path from their lips to their chin. But they didn't smell bad, just musty like you would expect an egg man from the country to smell.

The milkman came twice each week and left milk in glass bottles. The cream rose to the top and filled the narrow neck. We had to shake the bottle to mix it back together. In the summertime the Good Humor man in his snowy white uniform came to the corner of 2nd Street and Sterling Avenue and jingled the bells on his truck. Children came scurrying from cracks and crevices, nooks and crannies, up and down the street to get in line for the frozen treats.

The fish man came by honking his horn on Fridays, and all the Catholic mothers came running to get their mackerel for Friday night's fish supper so the family could escape mortal sin. In those days if we Catholics knowingly ate meat

It'll Be Okay In The Morning

on Friday, it was considered a mortal sin, and God forbid you should die with that sin our your immortal soul. If you did, you would be condemned to the everlasting fires and burn in hell for eternity. Times have changed though. God has softened. I guess He felt that hell was a pretty stiff penalty for consuming a hot dog on a Friday. So God told the Pope to back off and lighten up. It's not a mortal sin any more. I can't help wondering what happened to all those poor souls over all those centuries who ate meat on Friday, died and went to hell. I wonder if they got a parole, and I wonder how God could ever make it up to them.

Refrigerators and washing machines were just becoming popular in those days. Not many families had them until after the war. Housewives washed their clothes by hand. Mom eventually got a washing machine, but she still had to feed the clothes through a ringer that came with the machine. Then she hung them out to dry on a clothesline that stretched 100 feet from our back porch to a tree across the hedge on the Beaumont's property next door.

Until the late 1940s, when we got a refrigerator, we had an icebox. The iceman came every few days with 30- or 40-pound blocks of ice to save our perishables.

We had a coal furnace to heat our home until 1948. A coalscuttle, like a screw conveyor, was supposed to feed it automatically, but it never worked very well, and Dad had a heck of a time trying to relight the darn thing.

We had two small grocery stores downtown, a mile or so from home. We had no supermarkets. We did a fair amount of shopping just up the street at our local Italian Mama and Papa stores, Toro's and Fatarola's. Neither old Mrs. Toro nor old Mrs. Fatarola could speak much English. They dressed alike in the same old shapeless, dark nondescript print dress that fit comfortably over their shapeless, nondescript torsos. They wore their heavily gray-streaked hair in a bun, sometimes with a hair net. The stores always smelled of something cooking in the back where they lived. It was mixed with a musty old store smell and the aroma of parmesan and provolone cheeses hanging in the front window.

There were other stores in the neighborhood: Nick the Butcher, Quadagno's Sundries and Charlie Puma's candy store. If we had a few pennies, we went to Charlie's and always overstayed our welcome, leering into the curved glass cases and inspecting the gallon-sized glass jars filled with penny candy, trying to decide what to buy.

Up on West Street in the woods behind the riding stable were hundreds of acres of wild woods. Some folks from across the tracks went trapping muskrat there. Deer, raccoon, possum, and an occasional fox shared the forest. It was an adventure to go exploring and pretending. "Shhh, What was that noise? I swear I saw a bear back there behind that tree—and—and an Indian too!"

Sometimes we risked the darkness of the unknown underworld and teased the poor souls resting in the old graveyard on West Street. We dared and double-dared each other to go on in there. "Chicckkken! There's nothing in there—just a bunch of DEAD PEOPLE. Go ahead! Go ahead! They can't hurt you—they're DEAD!" No one wanted to be the first to chicken out. So someone would always take the dare, and the rest of us would follow. We shinnied through the gap in the three-foot-high fieldstone wall. The graveyard wasn't kept very well. Weeds and vines grew up around old tilted and fallen headstones where time had all but erased the names. But we could still read most of them, some dating back to the 1600s.

It'll Be Okay In The Morning

We imagined all kinds of things about that graveyard, the people buried there, how they must have lived—and died. And sometimes I would lie awake at night frightened of something about that place but unable to see it clearly.

When the interstate highway came through Harrison, they had to dig up all those graves and move them. We wondered if the people buried there would get angry or get lost. I had some bad dreams about that, too.

We had brooks with frogs and crawfish hiding under rocks and a real old swimming hole where "Boys Only" went skinny-dipping on hot summer days. There was no TV, no video games, no computers, no Game Boys. We didn't need them. We were better off without them. It was a great time for growing up.

God blessed Harrison.

Chapter 4.
Bruce

My brother, Bruce, was born in July 1938; the first-born son of an Old World Italian father. For Bruce it was an honor and a burden. Serious and studious, handsome and talented, he was everything his parents could want in a son. Why Mom and Dad had any other children is a question. It may have just been a matter of God's will—a dubious reward for not practicing birth control. It's possible my sister and I are mistakes of passion. My dad had a libido big enough for mention in *Guinness Book of World Records*. Unfortunately, he wasn't all that considerate of Mom, and his romantic skills were quite lacking. It was a problem for both of them.

Dad died fifteen years ago, but that libido may have survived somewhere on its own.

Bruce was showered with accolades and expectations. I got neither, and there was always a tension between Bruce and me. It was all too obvious that Bruce was top dog. It didn't seem fair that just because he was born first he was loved so much more.

I wanted equal time and recognition. But when the odds were clearly against getting it, I stopped trying. I gave up until I was 22 and felt able to succeed on my own merits. I finally gave up being jealous and envious and led my own life. Bruce and I don't talk much any more. We really haven't in ten years now. Maybe we never did.

Sometimes I miss my brother, but life is a little more peaceful this way. It's the best thing.

Chapter 5.
The Spencer Pharmacy

Dad opened the Spencer Pharmacy in 1940, and in October of that year I was born. He indulged Mom, and I got an Irish first name, Brian, after the great Celtic king, Brian Boru. It was a hard name to live up to, and I was to fall a little short for a good part of my life.

In the 1940s pharmacies were small, one-man businesses. There were no Walgreen's or Rite Aids. All Dad's customers knew him. The pharmacist was a man to be trusted as much as a priest or doctor. For many of the poor Italian immigrants who didn't speak English, Dad was their doctor and maybe even a priest for a few.

The Spencer Pharmacy was 25 feet wide and 160 feet deep with one big glass front window displaying two giant red and green apothecary jars. It was an "ethical" pharmacy, which meant Dad sold little else other than pharmaceuticals, prescriptions, medical equipment and supplies.

There were big glass cases that lined 50 feet of the store and displayed a variety of medical devices—crutches, and canes, elastic bandages and elastic stockings, back braces and bed pans and trusses. There was some room for non-ethical items in the store—perfumes and powders, boxed Whitman Chocolate Samplers, a six-foot freezer chest for Louis Sherry fine ice cream. But there was no soda fountain and no newspapers or magazines for sale in Dad's store.

Toward the back of the store was a five-foot high wall topped by a six-inch high piece of glass that Dad peered through to see who had come in. In those days pharmacists made many of their prescriptions from scratch, and the wall preserved the sterile sanctity of Dad's secret preparations—as well as the view of last night's left over cold pizza and the empty bottle of Heineken.

Customers entering the store might catch a whiff of some exotic potion or poultice being whipped up in the back room, wintergreen, camphor, eucalyptus. Or they might gag on the smell of sulfa drugs Dad concocted for acne; yellow, rotten-egg smelling glop for unfortunate teens who slathered it on their zit-covered, pock-marked faces. Dad actually used mortars and pestles and vernier scales, test tubes and Bunsen burners. These are just decorative memorabilia today. He even had his own suppository machine.

As we grew older, we were expected to help at the store by sweeping, mopping, washing the glass cases and sometimes waiting on customers. Dad's most popular item was something called terpin hydrate with 2% codeine. It was a cough medicine. It tasted like turpentine, but no matter; it was great stuff! If it didn't stop the coughing, you didn't care. Dad sold it by the case. He told us to come and get him if anyone asked for it. And a lot of old down and outers were regulars. I don't think you can buy it any more. We also called Dad whenever someone asked for a pack of Trojans. When I was ten, I knew what the customer was going to do with them, but I didn't understand why.

The Spencer Pharmacy was Pete's pride and joy, next to his first-born son. He spent 13 hours per day, six days per week in the store and from 8:00 am until 1:00 pm on Sun-

It'll Be Okay In The Morning

days. He rarely took a vacation. He preferred the store; it was not just his business; it was his escape.

The little storefront pharmacy became more like home than his real home, complete with every comfort and convenience: refrigerator, freezer, radio, stove, coffee maker and, in time, a television. He had the convenience of Charlie Kahn's Delicatessen next door, Shopwell supermarket and Risoli's Italian Restaurant and Pizzeria within easy walking distance. Sometimes he had Mom bring his meals down to the store. He was happily busy. He didn't spend much time with us or with Mom.

The pharmacy was the hang out for some of Harrison's characters: Old Mr. Policritti with his thick Italian accent, basso profundo voice and natty suspendered attire. He sat in the big wooden chair Dad placed just inside the door so older folks could rest. Mr. Policritti greeted people in perfect Italian or very broken English, holding his ivory-headed cane between his knees, hands folded on top.

Then there was Raspberry. It was the only name anyone knew him by. He was supposed to be a WWI war veteran, but no one really knew. Rassie had a toothless grin and a pronounced stutter. He entertained us kids by engulfing his nose with his lower lip and rolling his eyes round and round. Rassie washed windows, mopped floors and ran occasional errands. He smelled like old dirty window washing water, but his clothes always looked clean. He lived in a basement room in the Calvert Apartments and died a very, very old young man.

All the priests of St. Gregory's Catholic Parish, including Bishop Dargin and all the nuns from the convent, patronized the Spencer Pharmacy. Dad, good Catholic that he was, gave them all whopping discounts that I'm sure paid his admission to heaven.

    His store was only one block from the police station, and one or another of the patrolmen were often found in the back room having a coke or a sandwich with Dad and maybe, much later, something a little stronger. There were some slower nights when the regulars—First Selectman Joe Fiore, Dad's friends Joe DelVecchio, Joe Blasi, Matty Delzio and Joe Vassalo and others—would order pizza from Rissoli's and play pinochle. On these nights customers were considered an intrusion. Life was fun at the store.

Chapter 6.
#3 Second Street— Home

With two little boys running around, our apartment was just too small. We needed a new home. Dad bought our first and only house from the Goldmans at # 3 Second Street. It was the house Mom and Dad would live in for the next 40 years; the house we would all grow up in; the house that would give us bad dreams and hide the embarrassing secrets of alcoholism and domestic abuse.

In the 1940s Second Street was mainstream middle class America. Cozy, modest homes of less than 2000 square feet on modest lots of less than ¼ acre. The neighbors were a comfortable mixture of European middle class: the Coulters, Scottish; the Norths, English; the Quinns, Clearys, Donovans and Drummonds, Irish; the Beaumonts, French; the Scarcellas, Pisanis and Vasallos, Italian. It was a wonderful neighborhood of good people, Old World and New.

We moved into our little brown stucco house in 1943. Climb seven brick steps to the simple front door. Enter into a tiny sun porch of a hundred little windows, a buffer of privacy from the few passersby. Three small bedrooms upstairs serviced by a single bathroom that never had a lock. And on top, capping the old house, a musty old attic, exposed rafters, dangerous undependable wide floor planking and a variety of trunks and boxes of treasures left behind by the Goldmans. Downstairs was a very unremarkable kitchen with a single hutch full of plain unmatched plates and a collection of jelly glasses. The living room of pale green stucco walls was barely big enough for a couch and chair, but Mom crammed it with a hodge-podge of tables and overstuffed easy chairs.

The centerpiece of the formal dining room was the old antique trestle-based dining table and chairs, falling apart but functional. And in the corner of the dining room, an out of place day bed for Mom's too-frequent, alcohol-induced afternoon naps. The whole house was decorated entirely by Mom in eclectic Irish: flowered wall papers in the bed rooms, doilies that nearly covered the holes in the arms of the overstuffed but leaking chairs, phony looking phony flowers, bric-a-brac memorabilia from New York and Atlantic City.

Downstairs under the house was the cold, damp, stone cellar. Dad spent a fortune finishing it in knotty pine, but it was still a cold, damp stone cellar. It looked like a cellar, smelled musty and dank like a cellar, and it filled with two or three feet of water whenever we had a serious rainfall.

Our house was within easy walking distance of everything we needed: school, church, Casa De Villa Pizzeria, Fatarolla's and Toro's Markets, Charlie's and Nick's candy stores. And with a little walking effort, to Dad's Spencer Pharmacy and the village shops and movie theatre, all within less than a mile.

Our first few years on Second Street were happy.

The neighborhood was a little boy's adventure land. Across the street from our house was a large rock formation rising about 40 feet above the street and a dirt driveway that led up to old Miss Bricker's garage. The top of the driveway ended in a wooded area with mysterious rock

It'll Be Okay In The Morning

outcroppings that ran alongside the New York/New Haven railroad line.

Off to the left was a small hill covered by a beautiful golden meadow with a few oaks and maples scattered here and there. The place earned the name Cosacchi's Mountain. It was probably no more than 50 acres, but it was anywhere we wanted it to be. It was a magic place. The Lone Ranger, Red Rider and Little Beaver, or marines fighting against the Japanese in the Pacific, Flash Gordon, The Green Hornet, the Evil Emperor Ming, Tarzan, King Arthur, Sky King, The Invisible Man; every super hero we knew or made up lived there. And on Cosacchi's Mountain the good guys always won.

It was the mid/late 1940s, the world was tired of wars and for a brief time there were none. We fought our battles with sticks and used our fingers as guns—simple little boy fantasy—always the triumph of good over evil!

We lived across the street from the railroad tracks. Commuter and freight trains rumbled by day and night, but we all got used to it. Even in the summer with all the windows and doors open I don't recall the trains as a distraction. And some nights when it was especially hard to get to sleep, the clickity-clack-bump-bump-rattle helped me drift off.

We played cops and robbers and cowboys and Indians on Cosacchi's Mountain with the Coulters, Bobby and Eddie Dean, weird Bill Weir and a few others. We organized an exclusive boys' club with a secret password and hiding places, and we all followed the exploits of our radio heroes.

And we built a clubhouse.

Brian Cosacchi

On the side of the small hill, in the middle of the sweet long grass meadow was an open area perfect for a dugout clubhouse. It would have to be a hole deep enough for us to stand in with a slight crouch and big enough for all seven or eight of us to fit. We dug in earnest and succeeded in building an underground fort. We found some wide planking for a roof and scattered clumps of grass on top so it blended well and disappeared into the little hill. A few of us appropriated candles and matches from our homes to give us super-secret, spooky shadow candlelight for our club meetings.

We filled the clubhouse with the best available comic books: Red Rider, The Green Lantern, Superman and Porky Pig. Wonder Woman, with her well-developed and prominently displayed female attributes, held very special appeal for us even at nine or ten years (although we weren't sure exactly why).

Some of us sold Northrup and Burpee flower seeds in the neighborhood from catalogs and accumulated points to get prizes like Wham-O sling shots and chemistry sets. We wrote away for special things we heard of on the radio, like secret decoder rings, secret compartment belt buckles and secret compass rings with whistles in them that glowed in the dark and smelled funny.

Mr. Dietz lived on the corner of First Street and Sterling Avenue. His house was in poor condition, with the siding falling off, paint peeling and the garage roof buckling. He lived alone. We all thought he was a little crazy, but we liked to hang around his house because he had the world's largest collection of pigeons, Blue Bars, Red Bars and Fan Tails, pigeons of every color. We all wanted pigeons too, but none of our mothers would let us have them except for Eddie Julian's mom. She let him have a half dozen. We were all jealous. Eddie let us come over to his house and watch his pigeons.

The Clearys lived around the corner near Mr. Dietz on Sterling Avenue. They had a vicious German Shepard. Every time we had to pass by their house on our bicycles, we cautiously, quietly approached, waiting for the moment when King saw or smelled us and attacked. At that instant our adrenalin kicked in like air sucked into a supercharger. We shifted into high gear and sped as fast as we could past the Cleary house. Gary Donovan didn't make it one day and had an awful chunk taken out of his leg.

A small group of us invented the game of Bicycle Polo played with a soccer ball or basketball. We used baseball bats for polo mallets and rode our trusty metal steeds with one hand while flailing at the ball with the other, occasionally crashing into each other but without any major injury.

In the summer, when we weren't at the beach or summer camp, we sold homemade lemonade on the corner. The neighborhood's parents were our best (sometimes our only) customers.

One summer we held The Cosacchi Carnival; a putting green on the impossibly rough grass along the woods, balloon darts, pitch penny and a House of Horrors. Bruce lay in wait in the attic of our garage with a sheet over his head and a noisemaker to terrify those who dared climb the rickety steps into the almost pitch-black sauna. Unsurpassed excitement, and for only a nickel!

And sometimes we played with matches!

Chapter 7.
Matches

Until 1948 there was no television in Harrison. Aside from radio and Saturday matinees there wasn't much manufactured entertainment. We created our own adventures and excitement with imagination. And sometimes we upped the ante, dabbling with the forbidden...playing with matches. There was an excitement about matches when we were children, a compulsion that was irresistible. When I was six or seven, before the Beaumonts built their house on the lot next door, I sneaked some matches from the house and took them to the empty lot to experiment. Matches were different then. You could scratch them on anything and they burst into flame. You didn't need the matchbox. It was like the cowboys in the old movies who scratched matches on their butt to light their cigarettes.

I piled up some dead grass, struck a match on a rock and fed it to the grass. It burned. I was transfixed and couldn't take my eyes off the growing flame. I added a small stick or two. It felt warm and was so beautiful. I added a few more small sticks. I didn't see a finger of the little fire reach out to tickle the dead grass and leaves to my right. I didn't see it until there was too much fire for me to stop it. I panicked and ran. Soon the smoke caught the attention of the neighborhood, and in no time at all the fire truck was there to put it out, thankfully before it got to our garage. I thought I got away with it, but I was frightened. So when Officer Bisceglia came with my father to ask me if I knew how the fire started, I held my breath. I said I didn't, but somehow I knew they knew, but they said no more. For weeks afterward I expected the police to come and arrest me. I worried about being sent to jail. They taught me a lesson even if they didn't know!

I was not the only one irresistibly drawn to matches. All the secret club members were too, including my brother Bruce. On one very dry, bright, sunny summer day several of us were playing by the clubhouse. Bored, we invented a disastrous new challenge game. You could call it "How far can you let the fire go?" or Chicken with fire. The rules were simple: Strike a match; Drop it in the tall dry grass and see how far you can let it burn before you put it out. The one who could let it burn furthest was the winner. On this day the unquestioned winner was Bruce.

After a few others chickened out, it was Bruce's turn. He struck the head of the wooden match on the side of the Blue Diamond cardboard matchbox. Its white tip flared to life. He didn't wait to watch it burn down to the wood. He dropped into the dry grass at its earliest, most powerful moment. It took just a second for the grass to give growing life to the little flame. It spread faster than any of us thought possible. It was Bruce's job to put it out, but it was quickly apparent to us all that he couldn't do it alone. We all tried jumping on the flames, but the jumping spread the fire and made it worse. We realized that while Bruce clearly won the contest, we all lost. The wave of fire spread and we scattered in all directions, every man for himself, running to hide and be somewhere else when the fire-truck came. The fire covered several acres by the time it was under control. It slightly scorched the side of old Mrs. Bricker's garage. This time officer Bisceglia made sure he found out how the fire started, and all the Cosacchi Mountain Club members got thrashings. It didn't stop us from stealing matches, but it sure made us more careful.

Chapter 8.
Roseanne Quinn

The three Quinn children lived a few houses up the street on Francis Avenue. Patty, the eldest, was about 9 or 10. She was sort of pretty. Roseanne was my age—about 7. She was skinny and plain looking, not pretty at all. Jimmy was their younger brother, and he was what we used to call retarded. We picked on Jimmy a lot, which was a bad thing to do, and I was always sorry afterwards. I made sure to include that as a bad sin in my weekly confession to Father Laffin.

One late afternoon when my mom's Cub Scout Den was meeting and Roseanne came down the street to watch, she and I went into our garage. I was too young to be a Cub Scout, but I was old enough to be aware of some differences between boys and girls. I had seen my little sister Sheila without her clothes on, and she didn't have a penis. But looking at Sheila when she was naked was boring. I wanted to find out what other girls looked like without their clothes on, and I really wanted them to see me without any clothes on too. So, I proposed to Roseanne that we show our private parts to each other. We each pulled down our pants and, still being too young to understand sexuality, we showed each other our rear ends. Then as we were about to turn, face each other and expose our real differences, Mrs. Quinn opened the garage door. There was shock and awe all around. I couldn't get my pants up fast enough. I'm not sure whether I was more embarrassed or frightened. I ran out the back door of the garage through the hedges and grape vines and the rusted barbed wire on the side of our property.

"Dad's going to kill me. I know he's going to kill me," I cried for just a minute, but I was too frightened to continue. I waited and waited and fretted. Hours passed. It was getting dark, and I was getting cold. I knew I had to go home. This running away stuff had never done me any good. It just made Dad madder. I was frightened and dejected. I thought to myself, *At least you could have asked someone pretty. She's not pretty.*

By the time I got home, it was dark. Dad was there. He jutted out his lower jaw and bit down on his upper lip so he looked like a bulldog. He always did that just before he pulled his belt off and started wailing away. I resigned myself to the imminent beating but was surprised that Dad didn't seem to have his heart in it. I survived, and the welts were gone in the morning.

I didn't speak to Roseanne much after that, and I never looked Mrs. Quinn in the eye again—ever.

Chapter 9.
My First Cigar

Dad was a Lucky Strike chain smoker. He had cigarettes stashed all over the house. Growing up, the smell of cigarette smoke was Dad's smell and it was everywhere. It never appealed to me, and the smell of the raw tobacco was repulsive. Cigarettes weren't interesting.

But my "Uncle" Nunzio Ricci smoked cigars. He had one going all the time, and the smell of his cigar and the kind of happy-go-lucky guy Uncle Nunzio was made cigars appealing.

One afternoon when Mom was again having one of her Cub Scout den meetings, I stumbled across a couple of cigars in one of the end tables in the living room. A little voice inside whispered, "Here's your chance. No one will ever know. Go ahead. Do it." I recognized the voice as the same one that told me to go into the garage with Roseanne Quinn. Why I didn't dismiss it I'll never know. I still hear that voice from time to time and still find it irresistible.

There was no one else in the house. I picked up a cigar and a book of matches from the drawer and sped up the stairs to the little bedroom where Mom slept. There was a space between the wall and the bed just big enough to squeeze into. I settled into the hiding place, held my breath and listened for a minute. The only sounds were of Mom's Cub Scout den playing outside.

I bit off the end of the cigar like I had seen Uncle Nunze do a hundred times. I struck the match, sucked in on the end of the cigar and drew the smoke into my mouth and into my lungs. It didn't taste as good as it smelled coming from Uncle Nunzio's cigar. It hurt and burned. I coughed and gagged a little and pushed out all the dark blue smoke that hadn't found a home in my lungs. "One more time," said the little voice. And even though I really didn't feel like it, "Aw go ahead, who knows when you'll ever have a chance to do this again?" I sucked in on the end of the cigar one more time and drew in the smoke. I looked up and standing there looking down over me was my little sister Sheila. "I'm telling on you. I'm telling Mom on you." I coughed and sputtered, trying to get rid of the smoke. I hadn't realized how much smoke and how much smell a cigar made in a little room like this. I stumbled to my feet from my cramped position, but Sheila had already disappeared. I began to chase after her, but after my first step the room begin spinning. I nearly fell down and felt like throwing up. I barely made it to the end of the hall and into the bathroom. As I knelt down by the bowl, I doused the cigar into the waiting water. It was shortly followed by a splash of vomit. I flushed, and the toilet bowl started spinning and I started sweating. I threw up more. I threw up everything I had ever eaten—everything I had ever drank.

I lay there for a short time thinking about dying. Then I remembered Sheila—that little *&$@##—going to tell Mom. Mom would be coming to kill me any minute. I'd better hide. But before I could get to my feet, the bathroom door opened and Mom stood there shaking her head. "I just got off the phone with your father. He can't close the store right now or he would come home and kill ya here. So, he wants ya to get on your tricycle and peddle down to the store so he can kill ya there. And you better be quick about it or he'll murder ya."

"What's the use?" I thought. I felt like dying anyway. By the time I got outside, Sheila had told all the Cub Scouts

It'll Be Okay In The Morning

what I had done. Most of them were laughing. A few, including Bruce, said nothing and looked sorry for me. Then, as I mounted my dilapidated, broken down big hand-me-down tricycle, Gene Fidelli came up to me. He held out his hand, "Here Brian, take this. It might save your life." Between his thumb and index finger he pressed a piece of clover. "It's a four leaf clover. It's supposed to bring you good luck. I just found it in your lawn. Here, take it." I think I said, "Thank you." I tucked it into my shirt pocket so as not to crush it and started peddling my last mile to the Spencer Pharmacy.

He can't kill me in front of his customers. He'll have to take me in the back room and kill me there. Maybe I should wait outside and go in with a customer. I stopped in front of the store. I couldn't believe I got there so fast. I parked my crummy old tricycle and walked in. *Let's get it over with,* I thought but didn't really mean it.

Out from behind the protective wall walked not Dad, but Uncle Nunze. *What's he doing here?* He smiled and laughed and reached out his arms, a cigar clenched in his teeth. "Brian! How're ya doin' buddy?" He laughed. I could see Dad through the glass. He looked like he was smiling. "What's that ya got there?" Uncle Nunze reached out toward my shirt and picked the four-leaf clover from my pocket. "Hey, Pete, he's got a four leaf clover." Dad looked up from his work. He DID smile, and he went back to work. Uncle Nunze looked down at me and glanced at his lit cigar and said, "Hey, I understand you like these too. How would you like one of mine?" And he reached into his vest pocket and pulled out a brand new one, wrapper and all. A weak smile said, "No thanks, Uncle Nunz."

There never was any further mention of the cigar incident. I started smoking them again about fifteen years later. And always whenever I find myself in the midst of a patch of clover, I bend and look and hope. But I've never found another.

Chapter 10.
Sheila

Life might have been easier when I was eight if I hadn't been cursed with a little sister. My brother Bruce and I were only two years apart. We played with all the other boys in the neighborhood. We got along well most of the time until he started liking girls. He didn't want me hanging around anymore after he started seeing, and probably kissing, Rene Brulatour.

But Sheila was almost four years younger than me, and a girl, and I didn't want her hanging around me! It was embarrassing. Every time I turned around, there she was, chubby little Sheila. She wanted to be with her big brother—to harass, provoke, incite, goad, prod, and tease, in that whiny crybaby pout, "I want to play tooooo! I'm going to tell Mooommmmy." She whined and threatened until I turned into a raging munchkin and attacked.

I pushed her to the ground—to the living room floor—wherever the rage took over. I pinned her chubby little arms with my knees and then inflicted outrageous torture. I positioned my head directly above her chubby face and snorted backwards, retrieving mucus and mingling it with saliva. Sheila could see what was coming and screamed and cried and violently jerked her head from side to side, anticipating, then trying to escape the dangling string of slime. Sometimes I was satisfied just to tease and recovered the sloppy string with a quick slurp. Sometimes not. Then Sheila turned red, barely able to catch her breath from crying as the slimy drool dropped onto her cheek or nose.

But the pleasure of revenge faded quickly and was replaced by guilt and regret. Guilt because of true remorse for having hurt another human being and regret because of the reprisal I was sure to suffer at the hands of my mother or father. Reckoning was always close at hand. I never learned.

If Mom felt she could catch me, she went outside, cut a green branch from the hedge that bordered our house, tracked me down, cornered me, and with a swoosh lay that switch across my young butt or legs. The blows stung and burned like fire and raised half-inch welts wherever she struck. The pain would last for hours; the marks, for days.

But Mom's punishment was the easy way out. If the offense was bad enough or if Mom couldn't catch me, she called Dad. He then had to close the pharmacy and come home to mete out punishment. The actual number of times Dad had to close the pharmacy to come home and restore order couldn't have been more than 10 in 10 years. It seems like a thousand—so vivid—always the same.

First the phone call to the store; Mom dialed Tennyson 5-1960. I could hear the voice on the other end answer, "Spencer Pharmacy." It was Dad's voice. I knew it would be, but hoped he was too busy to answer (or maybe dead). He never was. The conversation was always brief, with Sheila's contrived melodramatic crying in the background. "Dad, I'm afraid you'll have to come home," Mom said. "They're at it again, and there's nothing I can do." A muffled response and Mom hung up the phone, turned to me and said, "Well you've done it now. Your father's had to close the store." I swear no sooner did the last word pass her lips than our car pulled up in front of the house.

It'll Be Okay In The Morning

Dad clambered from the car up the seven brick steps into the sun porch. The glass door with the Venetian blind crashed open. There he was, nostrils flared, breathing heavily, always biting his upper lip with his lower teeth like a bulldog. "okay," he yelled to Mom, "where is he?" She didn't answer. I was right there. He was looking right at me. Even as he was asking where I was, he was pulling his belt from around his waist. One smooth quick motion like a Samurai drawing his sword.

How many times can you raise and swing a belt from left to right, then back from right to left in one minute? Dad must be in the Guinness Book. The belt was a blur as it struck, barely slowing as it arced up in the opposite direction and down again faster than the eye could follow. I closed my eyes, yelled and cried, "Please No Dad, I'm sorry. I won't do it again." Boy, what a licking! And through my tears and crying, did I see Sheila smirking? Dad went back to the pharmacy. Life returned to normal.

Chapter 11.
Winter

The radio announcer spoke softly "This is WFAS and WFAS FM in White Plains, New York. Nearly a foot of snow fell on Westchester County last night. Here is the list of school closings we have received thus far:"

It was 6:45 in the morning, pitch dark outside, and we had been awake since 5:30 waiting for this announcement. We were in bed in our pajamas listening and looking out the window into the winter morning. What little light leaked through the clouds teased the night, giving us brief glimpses of the snow flakes falling, fluttering, floating slowly, softly to the ground. Such sweet silence!

The announcer continued, "Rye High School...And in Harrison," we held our breath, "Saint Gregory the Great School, Harrison Avenue School, the High School and Parsons Memorial will all be closed today."

No school! Elation! Euphoria! A foot or so of snow on the ground, and, in the growing gray light, we could see it was still coming down! Dad had already been awake for some time and had turned up the thermostat on the new oil burner. The old radiators were cheering, "Clankity, clank. No school!" We might have gone back to sleep, or tried to. But we only pulled the heavy blankets up over our heads, snuggled up with our pillows leaving just our noses exposed to sniff the delicious cold air that slipped under the small crack Mom left in the bottom of the window to feed us fresh air.

(Mom believed in fresh air for everything. She hung out the laundry in the freezing fresh air. Sometimes we helped her bring in the frozen line of clothes to stand next to the radiator, slowly thaw, relax then collapse. I loved the way they smelled still cold and fresh.)

By 7:15 we were up scurrying about looking forward to the hot breakfast Mom fixed on such a special cold morning: Aunt Jemima Pancakes with gobs of butter, Log Cabin maple syrup and a cup of coffee. We gobbled the sweet sticky calories and felt warm inside, and Mom made sure we stayed warm, bundling us in snowsuits like little Michelin men. We rushed to put on our rubber galoshes, wrestling with the buckles, trying to slip the little metal tab into the correct little metal slot—not too tight—not too loose, frustrated by all that wasted time!

Finally, I opened the front door. The sun had come out, and the brightness shocked my eyes shut. I peeked with one, then the other, and adjusted to the blazing light ricocheting from the unspoiled snow. The plows hadn't reached Second Street yet, and just a few cars had left their tracks. It was hard to tell how deep the snow was. It mounded on our front steps like layers on a wedding cake, but was so light that it lifted and flew from under my feet as I put my foot down. The bottom three steps were totally covered, and as I stepped to where I thought the ground should be, the snow rose up to my waist. I plowed forward excited, laughing, happy, looking forward to new adventures.

We became entrepreneurs going door to door with shovels in hand, looking cute and strong and irresistibly pathetic. We promised our neighbors to do great work shoveling walks and driveways for the unbelievably low price of 50 cents—a dollar if you were rich. Most of the neighbors knew us. All were good Christians and couldn't say no to

It'll Be Okay In The Morning

the bunch of Our Gang ragamuffins dressed in Michelin Tire snowsuits—and we did a very good job.

The morning passed with the sun dancing on the frozen white ocean. By noon Bruce and I had earned several dollars shoveling, and most of the remaining neighbors had long since shoveled themselves out and left for the day. Now we could do the things little boys should do on beautiful, bright, snow-covered days.

Mom gave us some hot soup for lunch, and we were off. We went looking for our sleds. Bruce had the prize, The Flexible Flyer he got for Christmas a year or two before. It was built low to the ground, not too big or too small, just right for maximum speed. The magnificent Flexible Flyer American Eagle logo was prominent in the middle of the centerboard, with a beautifully varnished glossy finish. She was a beauty. Lots of the kids had Flexible Flyers. The kids who didn't, like myself, wished we had one. I had a boring, blah, plain wooden Western Auto sled. Its runners were too high, it was too big and clumsy, and down the center in bright red letters were the uninspired words "Western Auto." But it was my sled, and I never admitted its failings any more than I would admit my own. As far as I was concerned my sled was as good as or better than any old Flexible Flyer, and I raced everyone to prove it.

We pulled our sleds out of the garage attic and steel-wooled the rust off the runners. The plows had cleared Second Street, leaving huge snow boulders piled into dirty white mountains at the foot of the long driveway that wound it's way up to Miss Bricker's garage on the side of Cosacchi's Mountain. But the plowman always left behind a compressed layer of icy snow so slick and slippery that it would carry our sleds a tenth of mile past the bottom of Mrs. Bricker's driveway and part way up the Francis Avenue hill.

Brian Cosacchi

We took a lot of chances. Our mothers didn't know until we showed up on the doorstep with a bloody nose, cut lip, broken finger, or some minor missing body part. We challenged each other, and we were constantly looking for ways to come just short of killing or maiming ourselves.

The double-decker airplane was the best; two sleds stacked perpendicular to each other with the pilot sitting on the top sled! The sleds had to stay together, balanced, without slipping about. Most of the time they fell apart. And if they didn't, as our rickety pretend B29's lumbered through the snow skies, we were attacked by Japanese Zeros waiting in the snow clouds along the hill. They flew in, grabbing runners and flipping the sled; pilot and bombardier tumbling from the snow sky. Occasionally speed demons and daredevils crashed into trees and parked cars. Some of the collisions resulted in broken bones or lacerations. No one wore helmets. Tommy Gray cut his head open once going under a car, but no one died (that I can remember).

To add to the challenge we built a jump about two-thirds the way down the hill. The jump was about three-feet high and carried the sled rider flying through the air ten feet or so before landing with a smashing, crunching crash, knocking the air from the rider. It was an event that always drew a crowd. What fun! We laughed as we shook off the pain, tried to breathe and lied, "That was easy. I dare ya to try it." We added to the challenge by pouring water on the jump at night as the temperature dropped, freezing it into a giant ice cube. It carried the rider close to the stratosphere, landing with a jolting, bone-crunching crash.

The best of us even tried the double-decker airplane off the ice jump! Most of the time we never got that far. I don't recall anyone ever landing in one piece. It may have happened. I never did. But then again no one died (that I can remember).

Chapter 12.
Radio

Before 1948 when television changed our lives, we spent afternoons and most evenings in front of the big wooden RCA console radio with it's amber-colored station dial and cathedral-shaped, fabric-covered speakers. Even before going off to kindergarten I'd wake up each morning and tune in Don McNeil and his Breakfast Club. I marched around the breakfast table with all the people on the show as they sang, "First call to breakfast! Philco call to breakfast!" In the afternoons I drifted off for a nap to Oxydol's Own Ma Perkins or the voice of the distinguished announcer introducing Our Gal Sunday, the story that asked the question, "Can this girl from the little mining town in the West find happiness as the wife of a wealthy and titled Englishman?"

I recall those naps were always cozy.

Radio poked and teased our imaginations and brought a menagerie of stories and characters to life right there in our living room. Saturday mornings were the best—Big John and Sparky was introduced by The Teddy Bears' Picnic, then Smilin' Ed and His Gang told stories of adventure and were constantly harassed by Froggy the Gremlin, plunking his magic twanger and growling, "Hiya, kids, Hiya, Hiya."

Radio gave us an early appreciation of classical music. I recall The Lone Ranger galloping into our living room to the finale of the *William Tell Overture*, with me and Tonto galloping right along with him. And there was Sergeant Preston of the Royal Mounted Police cruising in with his husky, King, on his dogsled to Reznicek's *Donna Diana Overture*. Liszt, Tchaikovsky and the rest of the 19th century music notables contributed themes and incidental music to many of our shows.

Blessedly, political correctness hadn't been invented; Irish, Italian, Jewish, Negro, Polish, we all took turns in the "barrel." All were fair game for gentle pokes in those more innocent days in Harrison, New York. Everyone took the ribbing in good humor although some may have chafed a bit. I really didn't know any Negroes except for Charlie Williams. He was the only Negro in our class, and he was just like the rest of us except black.

Radio went its way even though some of our best radio friends made their way to television. Without the need any longer for an imagination, the characters in the flesh couldn't live up to the hero images we created.

Chapter 13.
TV

We owned the first TV in town. I was eight years old. Dad drew the winning ticket in the Knights of Columbus raffle. Dad happened to be the Grand Knight that year, and some people might have felt that his luck received more than a divine assist.

The year was 1948, and there was very little to watch during the day other than the test pattern on channel 5, the DuMont Television Network. The black and white striped Maltese Cross pattern filling the tiny 10 inch screen was accompanied by a calming single "ooooooooooooooo" sound. At first we were spellbound and just sat staring. We had never thought much about the magic of radio, maybe because it had always been there in our life, or maybe because it was only sound. But this! A real picture! It was exciting.

There were shows that we looked forward to each week, especially Howdy Doody and Buffalo Bob Smith and all the wonderful fantastic goofy characters that made Doodyville our own neighborhood: Mister Bluster, Clarabelle the Clown, Flubba Dub, and Princess Summer Fall Winter Spring. Mr. Bluster was always thinking up some sinister plot. Clarabelle sneaked around with his seltzer bottle hoping to get a clear shot at Buffalo Bob, but his schemes were foiled by the screams of the kids in the Peanut Gallery: an audience of 50 or 60 hysterically hollering children. Howdy was the hero, cleverly thwarting the villains.

Each Sunday in the early evening we watched Claude Kirchner's *Super Circus*: jugglers, acrobats, ponies and dog acts. It was not much of a circus, really. But there was Mary Hartline the *Super Circus* Band leader. I was only ten, but I confess I watched to ogle Mary Hartline in her white boots, golden blonde hair and gorgeous legs uncovered to the hip. She pranced about swinging her booty and baton, winking at the camera and all of us in TV land pretending to lead the band. I was a little embarrassed at my pre-adolescent gawkings and glanced away now and then to reflect an air of indifference.

Soon TV spawned a kaleidoscope of memorable characters and programs that have gone on to the great kinescope library in the sky: Milton Berle and Ed Sullivan, Rootie Kazootie, Winky Dink, Pinky Lee, Soupy Sales and dozens of others. In a year or two TV was 24/7. By 1950 all the New York baseball teams had their games televised.

Chapter 14.
The Big Game

We were all fanatic baseball fans following our favorite professional team. Most of the kids in the neighborhood were New York Yankee fans. The Coulters were exceptions, rooting for the New York Giants. And Dad and me were the odd couple praying for and placing our faith in The Brooklyn Dodgers. With affection they were called the "Brooklyn Bums" because they never failed to disappoint their loyal fans. I collected all their baseball cards, memorized their names and positions and could tell you the batting averages of the starting line-up. But year after year our "Bums" let us down, never able to win the "Big One"—the World Series. Oh, they got there often enough: 1947, 1949, 1952 and 1953. They won the National League Pennant four out of six years—a remarkable record! It's only more remarkable that they never won the World Series in all those chances. Even worse, every one of those losses was at the hands of the Damn Yankees. I felt I was wearing a humiliation sign around my neck: "loser." I got tired of saying wait 'till next year.

But 1951 was the worst. The Dodgers were riding high as August came around. It was the home stretch. Things would be different this year.

My Dodgers were far ahead in their National League Pennant race. They could cruise home, a whopping thirteen games ahead of the second place Giants on August 11. Only a month or so to go to complete the 156 game season. No one could catch us, and we just knew we would go on to win our first World Series. All those years of disappointment and ridicule at the hands of the Yankees and Giants would be erased.

Then something happened. Hardly noticeable at first, certainly no cause for concern as my Dodgers dropped a few games and the Giants began to close the gap. We still smiled and taunted the Coulters and the few other Giant fans in town. I went to my dad's pharmacy after school, and we watched the afternoon games on the little 11 inch screen. Between customers we commiserated and assured each other the Dodgers were okay.

Then, as the season came closer to the end, a sense of panic set in. Were we to be the brunt of jokes again? The Giants had closed the gap. Our neighbors the Coulters began to smile just a little. They were Presbyterian and Scottish. It was a small, superior, "its already been decided up there" sort of smile. Surely God wouldn't let the Protestants win.

It came down to the last game of the season. If the Dodgers lost and the Giants won there would have to be a best-of-three play off. And so it was that the Giants won in Boston, and my Dodgers lost in Philadelphia. There would be a play off.

Hope springs eternal, and we were the better team even though the Giants had won 37 of their last 45 games, an incredible 82%. Sure they had momentum, but we had "the boys of summer:" Campy, Row and Hodges, Snider and Furillo and Reese and Robinson to name a few.

The two teams split the first two games, and it came down to the final game in the best of three series. My Dodgers had a comfortable lead going into the ninth inning, 4 to

It'll Be Okay In The Morning

1. Then the Giants scored a run and left two men on base, 4 to 2. Bobby Thompson came to bat. He had two hits already in the game. Dad and I looked at each other both of us thinking, "Uh oh," and we held our breath. The customers out front in the store could wait!

We squinted and drew a deep breath as we watched relief pitcher Ralph Branca wind up and throw the first ball to Thompson. Strike one right down the pipe! "okay, okay, just take it easy!" Here comes the second pitch. High and inside. Ball one. I squinted my eyes tighter so that I could hear better. Then the third pitch. I heard a roar and Russ Hodges, the announcer yelling. He yelled and yelled and yelled the same thing over and over. Through my squint I had watched that third pitch jump off Bobby Thompson's bat and fly down the short left field line only thirty feet from "foul." But it wasn't. It sailed into the left field stands just 279 feet from home plate. Russ Hodges was yelling, "The Giants win the pennant, the Giants win the pennant, the Giants win the pennant!" I couldn't believe God would let this happen! I would never hear the end of this from Roland and Kenny Coulter. Maybe God was a Protestant after all.

Chapter 15.
Being Catholic

We were good Catholics. At least Dad and us kids were. Mom only went to church on special occasions. We went every Sunday and all 14 Catholic Holy Days of Obligation. In high school I was even more Catholic, making the nine first Fridays several times and once, the 10 first Saturdays. I was desperately devoted to my religion until I was 17 when I lost 40 pounds and met Kathy Crowley. But that's another story.

As children we attended St. Gregory the Great Roman Catholic Church. It was a basement church, all that was left of the original that had burned down long before I was born. During Mass all the children were seated in the front row so we could see the show. I had no idea what was going on up there on the altar, but I knew it was important. And I knew that I mustn't ever sit back and rest my rear end on the edge of the bench behind me. Instead I was taught by the good Sisters that, no matter how uncomfortable, I was to kneel erect with my back straight. If it hurt, we were told to "offer it up," meaning tough it out as penance for our sins.

When I turned seven, I received intense indoctrination into the faith to prepare for my First Communion. I didn't understand what that was, but I knew it was important. The Sisters told us it would bring us closer to God. Things weren't so good at home so the thought of getting closer to God was appealing. After Mass we were taken into the church hall and received our Catechism instruction. We had to learn all the answers to the questions we would be asked, or we wouldn't be able to receive the Host, the little white wafer that the priest turned into Christ's body during the Mass. At Communion everybody got to eat one. I learned all the proper answers to the proper questions: "Who made you?"..."God made me;" "Why did God make you?"..."To know, love and serve him." I was very good at it.

The last hurdle before I got to eat the Body of Christ was to make my first confession. Catholics believe they free their souls from the burden of sin by confessing their sins to a priest. The priest acts a surrogate for God, dispensing forgiveness for the truly contrite and admonishing and imposing penance as he sees fit in the name of God. For me, at seven, entering that dark closet-like confessional for the first time, I asked myself, "What should I confess?" At seven there really wasn't much. I thought through the Ten Commandments but couldn't think of anything except the way I tortured Sheila. I couldn't tell him that, and I was already sorry. So I made up some stuff so Father Laffin would be satisfied and have something to give me penance for. He was a good guy, and I knew he would know it was me, even through that black screen that separated us. In due course I received my First Communion. I understood what was going on up there on the altar, and I was happier knowing God was now my good friend.

Chapter 16.
Altar Boys

Shortly after my First Communion I was recruited to be an altar boy. My brother Bruce had been an altar boy for a year. Altar boys helped the priests with the Mass, handing them the wine and water, lighting the candles and ringing the bells every time they said "Sanctus" during the Mass. We had to memorize the whole Mass in Latin. We didn't have to know what all those words meant, but we had to say the words right. I studied very hard. I was afraid if the words didn't sound right, the Mass wouldn't count and the people would go to hell because the Mass wouldn't be official and I would go there too. So I memorized how it all sounded, *ad deam qui laetificat juven tutem meam—qui facit chelum ad terrum*. I learned it all. My debut was a success.

The whole thing was very mysterious, magic, solemn, quiet and a little scary because when Father Laffin or Father Prunty leaned over that big gold cup filled with those little hosts and said the magic words, "Hoc est enim corpus meum," the tiny pieces of bread were no longer just tasteless, impossibly flattened little wafers. They were now the actual, real flesh of Jesus. So we had to be very careful when we received Communion. And when Father put that body of Christ on my tongue I was taught never to chew it. So I would stick it on the roof of my mouth. Sometimes my mouth was a little too dry and I would have a devil of a time peeling it off with my tongue so that I could swallow it. But I never chewed it because chewing would definitely have hurt Jesus.

Serving Mass was not just a Sunday thing. Many weeks during the year Dad would roll me and/or Bruce out of bed at 5:30 to serve the 6:00 am Mass all week before going to school.

Easter week was a special week of "offering it up." That's the week that Christ died for us all on the cross. The special events began before the sun came up with the 5:00 A.M. Holy Thursday service to commemorate the Saints. The ritual culminated with chanting of the Litany of Saints. It was mystical but boring listening to the reading in Gregorian chant sung a little off key by Father McNulty. There were some Saints with really weird names like Saint Aphrodisius or St. Apollinaris Syncletica, and there were a bunch who had the same name. There must have been hundreds of Marys and Peters and Alexanders and Josephs. All in all there are about 10,000 Catholic Saints so they must have picked just the best ones for the Holy Thursday service. I hope the ones who got left out weren't offended. Anyway, the list went on for a couple of hours. Sometimes one of the altar boys would just keel over and one of the Priests would pick him up and carry him back into the sacristy. I used to envy those kids—even considered faking it. But I never did. My back still gets stiff recalling.

On and on and on it went. I followed along, humming the responses to keep myself awake and checked off the alphabet as they sang from Santa Augustina through Santa Dominca. When they reached Santa Michaela, I sighed, "Ah! Halfway. Relief!" The second half of the alphabet went faster as there were very few Qs', no Saint X's and the final "Y's" went very quickly. It ended with the lighting of the Pascal Candle. Then Dad took me to Cappy's Diner for soft-boiled eggs, toast and coffee.

It'll Be Okay In The Morning

Some mornings we got out of school to serve funeral masses. I liked getting out of school, but funeral masses were always scary. There was the coffin sitting right there in the middle of the aisle on top of some collapsible accordion set of rollers. There we were at the altar, looking out at the family and friends of the dead person. We all stood there facing the coffin, the priest and us two altar boys. The priest said some nice things I never really heard because I was thinking about who was in there. *I wonder what the dead person looks like. I wonder how he died? What would happen if the person wasn't dead at all and was in there by mistake? What if we saw a hand come out of the coffin or heard him knocking from inside? Would we all pretend not to hear it? What if they died of something catching? When I go down there with the incense could I still catch it and then die?*

Then the really scary part began. The altar boys carried either the holy water or the incense burner, the thurible used in the ceremony. The priest stepped down from the altar, and one of us followed first with the incense then the other with the holy water. We had to march once around the casket with the priest waving the incense back and forth over the casket or sprinkling it with holy water. I held his vestments up as we walked, thinking, *What if my cassock gets caught on one of the handles? What if I get stuck here? What if I accidentally pull the casket off the stand and it falls off and the coffin opens and the dead body falls out on top of me? I wonder if they will expect me to pick it up and put it back? What if I scream and it comes alive and laughs and strangles me?* It was all scary and distressing. I did not like serving funerals except when it was during school so I would get out of school for a few hours.

I liked serving weddings, though, because the pretty brides were always nice to look at, and at the end of the service the Best Man always came back and gave each of the altar boys a couple of dollars.

Chapter 17.
The Water Rats of Oakland Beach

"Ta tada tah!" Hands cupped around our mouths, faces lifted toward the sun, we trumpeted our fanfare, "Ta tada dah!" Fair warning given, we emerged from below the sand dunes to wreak havoc on unsuspecting infidels. The scourges of summer, The Water Rats of Oakland Beach, were loose again. No fair maiden would be spared. Repeating our battle cry, we swooped down, flying across the sands like the wind, beach towels for Bedouin capes secured about our necks with simple bulky half hitches floating in the wind behind us. I sped across the burning Sahara and singled out the most beautiful unsuspecting maiden sunning herself, relaxed, unaware of the impending attack. I spurred my Arabian stallion, and we galloped toward our victim. Only at the last instant did I deftly pull the reins left or right, leaving a cascade of sand splashing over my bewildered beauty. On I rode with my cohorts, righting imagined wrongs, impressing young women with gallant deeds and horsemanship. In time I rested, stabling my steed back in my imagination, settling down next to Mom with a glass of iced tea and a tuna sandwich. And then, a well deserved rest under the motley beach umbrella, a soft towel covering my back and legs, drifting off to my netherworld to the chatter of Mom and the Coulters and the Marcis discussing life.

We were the Water Rats. A wild bunch of 8- to 12-year-old urchins congregating each summer from 1947 until 1952 at Oakland Beach in Rye, New York.

Brian Cosacchi

We could swim faster and farther than the other kids. We knew where the best clamming was. We could pick up horseshoe crabs and spider crabs and blue shell crabs with impunity. We knew how to get under the boardwalk at Playland and scavenge for coins dropped by pedestrians above intended for the various vending machines. We disregarded most of the beach rules. They didn't apply to us. It was our beach. The "Keep off the Rocks" sign painted in ten-foot high letters on the huge sea wall was a warning about the danger the tides, currents and innocent looking waves posed. We never minded. The sea wall was no danger to us, and at high tide we swam the ¼ mile with our fishing drop lines tucked into our bathing suits. We played hide and seek among the boulders and fished for bergalls, little boney, spiny inedible fish that were easy and fun to catch.

We had summer snowball fights using small, harmless, translucent jellyfish instead of snowballs. These harmless hydroids invaded the waters of Long Island Sound by the thousands and were easily scooped up, one or two at a time. We flung them at each other. They landed on our bare flesh with a splat. We broke into teams and attacked each other, splat, splat, splat, and an occasional gulp, if a player couldn't keep his mouth closed.

We became entrepreneurs. Clamming was outlawed in Long Island Sound because of pollution and fear of contamination. But the law didn't apply to us nor a small group of old Italian beach goers. These older folks ignored the law and performed their clamming hula at low tide, shuffling their feet and swinging their hips from side to side, arms akimbo in waist high water digging with their feet for hard shell and cherry stone clams. But these were old folks. It was a challenge for them to dredge up a dozen clams in an hour or so, barely enough for their evening's linguine. We Water Rats saw the business opportunity and soon discovered the mother lode of clams resting just off our float in only 7 feet of water. The clams propagated there in profusion. We dove off the float into the soft mucky bottom and groped with both hands searching for the smooth, hard edges of the clams that lay just an inch or so below the surface of the muck. We became expert in picking out the live clams from the dead ones and the occasional rock and harvested as many as eight or ten clams in a single dive. My own record: a bathing suit stuffed with a full dozen. We sold our clams for a dime apiece or a dollar a dozen.

These were halcyon latency years, preteen years. Feelings about girls were changing. "I hate 'em." "I love 'em." "I love to hate 'em." "I hate to love 'em." Hate to hate. Love to love. At ten I could feel the stirrings—the rumbling percolating in my core like magma looking for a way out. I liked looking at girls but would deny it—suppress it. I risked sneak peeks and touches. Sometimes I would venture into the crowded shallow waters and dive beneath the surface with my face mask on to get a better look at all those legs and other female body parts and maybe accidentally gently bump against their smoothness. The volcano was growing. All of a sudden I liked fighting with girls and, most astounding, I liked losing. I liked starting fights with Nancy or Iris Howell and having them pin me to the ground. Those "stirrings" would find their way to my sensitive parts. It felt very good. And, even at 10, I wanted more, although I didn't know why.

Chapter 18.
Boy Scouts, Camp Siwanoy and The Order of the Arrow

I never got to be a Cub Scout. My brother Bruce was, and my Mom was a Den Mother. I was only seven, too young. At Den meetings I sat on the sidelines alone, watching the activities, wishing I could join in. When Bruce was eleven, the official age of entry, he joined the Boy Scouts. My Dad was friends with the Scout Master, and so a year later, when I was only ten, I was shanghaied into the Boy Scouts of America. With a little reluctance, I became the youngest, smallest member of Harrison's St. Gregory the Great Boy Scout Troop Number Two. Troop Two was well known among the five or six troops in Harrison. Our Scout Master was Norman Wurtzberger, a giant figure of an ex-Marine. Norm (we were allowed to call him Norm) demanded discipline and order in our meetings with a palpable "or else" doled out with a swagger stick he slapped against his trousers and sometimes across the backs of our legs. Almost everyone in Troop Two was from Harrison's Italian roots. They looked the part, and their names said it all: Wussie Basso, Pickles Rudolpho, Fats Solazzo, Blackie Castiglia, Chi Chi Galiulo, Richie Palazzola, the Modugno twins. We were all Italians, *Gumbas*, and proud of it. No one gave us any trouble.

Each year two Courts of Honor were held in Harrison to bestow ranks and merit badges on deserving scouts.

The highlight of the event was a drill competition to test the discipline and marching precision for each troop. We never looked as spiffy as the other troops; our company was made up mainly of the sons of blue-collar craftsman. Our uniforms were faded and mismatched, but we never lost a drill competition.

There was a price for joining Troop Two. Each new scout had to endure one or a series of somewhat uncomfortable initiations. Most popular among these were:

The Pink Belly: A group activity in which the new scout was held down by as many as necessary. The subject's belly was then exposed and the remaining brothers would slap the victim's tummy with their open hands until it turned the brightest red.

The Colgate Smile: The recruit was subdued, his pants removed, a tube of toothpaste (preferably Colgate for some reason) inserted and emptied into the rectum. The results were supposed to be similar to a Fleet's Enema but with a special toothpaste kick.

The Snipe Hunt: During a campout, a naive novice would be taken into the dark woods far from camp and told the objective of the evening was to catch the elusive snipe, an animal presumed to be a flightless bird. He was given a burlap bag and told that the rest of the troop would fan out and drive the snipe into his waiting bag by beating the bushes and yelling. At first the yelling and banging out there in the darkness was reassuring, but it soon faded then stopped and the night grew darker and the night sounds were strange and grew louder. It was a scary night for the novice. All the initiated had a good laugh at the new guy's expense.

It'll Be Okay In The Morning

There was one more initiation called. "Brown Balls" that involved brown shoe polish and the individual's testicles. No further description is warranted.

Being the youngest and smallest, it would seem I would be a prime target for all these initiations, but I knew I was the most vulnerable. So, from the beginning I developed a canny sense. I never received nor administered an initiation.

Camp Siwanoy was located 35 miles north of Harrison in the little town of Wingdale, New York. Wingdale's only notoriety was that one of New York's largest mental institutions was located there.

The Boy Scout Camp consisted of open-windowed wooden cabins and platform tents organized into 5 tribes of about 40 scouts each.

For me, these days at Siwanoy were the happiest of my life. I swam, boated, canoed, hiked, learned astronomy, studied reptiles and Indian lore and life saving and so much more. We were on the move all day, six days every week. At night we listened to Taps, and it was easy to drift off in the fresh air. Sometimes the rain sang me to sleep, accompanied by the night sounds. I never wanted to go home and cried that first year when Mom and Dad came to pick up me and Bruce.

The Order of The Arrow was a very special fraternity. Scouts were chosen by their peers and scout leaders. Tap out ceremonies took place every four weeks during the summers at Camp Siwanoy and captured the little boy imagination of everyone in attendance.

On these special nights the 250 scouts and some 50 visitors gathered in silence in the dark at the edge of the lake. Not a word, no sound until, breaking through the stillness, came a single voice chanting an invocation to Manitou, the greatest of American Indian Gods. The sound drifted to us from across the lake a quarter-mile away. My eyes searched the darkness for some sign of what might follow, but nothing was given away. Then, straight ahead across the lake a fire bloomed, breaking the night and revealing the silhouette of the praying Indian, arms upraised, outstretched, entreating Manitou. The Indian was as real as the fire, and every little boy standing by the water felt the magic of the night.

From the fire's light we watched five more Indians join him. Then, even from so far away, we could see each brave light a torch and quietly enter the water. They began swimming together across the still lake. Their torches raised, they paddled with their free arms, kicking without disturbing the water's surface. There wasn't a sound. Their rhythmic breathing barely touched the silence. As they drew closer to the center of the lake, unbelievably, a second fire grew up from the water itself, illuminating three more braves with torches standing on a raft. They entered the water, quietly, effortlessly joining their brothers. They all reached our shore together and approached a fire pit that had been prepared. They stabbed their torches into the waiting timber, exploding a blaze that in turn stabbed the darkness, illuminating the waiting congregation.

We could see these Indians clearly now, and although they looked like the camp counselors we worked and played with each day, we had no doubt that these truly were Delaware Indians, with their head dresses, paint, moccasins and ankle bells. And there was still not a sound from any scout or visitor.

It'll Be Okay In The Morning

Now the tap out. The braves fanned out and began running back and forth behind the long line of scouts and visitors looking for the inductees. We all knew what was about to happen, and while we hoped to be among those tapped that night, our desire was softened with the knowledge of what the next 24 hours would bring those chosen. I listened, never daring to look over my shoulder. I could hear ankle bells and moccasin-softened running footsteps behind me. The tapping began. The braves identified those chosen and shoved them forward from behind with such force that they were driven to their knees. Then they were picked up by the arms and dragged to the fire, so close that they had to take great care to protect faces and hair from the heat and embers that rifled from the blaze.

Then it was over. Ten individuals sitting, roasting in front of the blazing fire. Their next 24 hours was spent in absolute silence working on back-breaking projects and nourished only by bread and water. The reward would be worth it: membership in this respected brotherhood. We, the somewhat relieved unchosen, were led back into the darkness away from the light of the adventure. The only sound was the snap and crackle of the still blazing fire. I thought one day I too would be chosen to be tapped, roasted and to endure. My turn did come at thirteen. The memory of those magnificent pageants will last my lifetime.

Chapter 19.
Piano Lessons

Bruce started playing the trumpet when he was seven, taking lessons from Mr. Kohler. As the eldest son in an Italian household it was expected he would do well. He knew it, and he did well.

When I was seven, it was decided that I would take piano lessons. I wasn't very interested in playing piano. I just wanted to play. But Dad and Mom, (mostly Mom), thought it was important that I too play an instrument. So, my first shot at becoming the next Horowitz began with Thursday afternoon lessons from Mrs. Halpin. I hated it. I hated the stupid songs. I hated practicing. I hated frumpy Mrs. Halpin. Sitting there staring at the chipped keys of our old upright, I kept thinking of all that time I could be outside on my mountain with the pirates, cowboys and super heroes. Whenever I could, I cut my practice short and sneaked outside. If I had to practice, I found it less painful to make up my own music rather than play the stupid "Tom Tom" song.

One day Mrs. Halpin gave me a new song to learn, *Swans on the Lake*. She told me there was a recital coming for all her students and that this was the song I was to play. Mom was very excited and became my jailer, making sure I practiced every day for half an hour. I couldn't escape, but I could still cut the practice short by a few minutes on either side. Sometimes Mom wasn't feeling well, and I could get away. But the upshot of my reluctance and conniving was that I didn't learn *Swans On The Lake* very well. Mrs. Halpin urged me to practice more. She said I wouldn't be ready for the recital if I didn't.

I didn't.

The evening of the recital came. I was ready. I knew the first part well, and that would be good enough. No one would notice the rest. All the other kids were just like me and no one would be perfect.

Mom parked the car in front of Mrs. Halpin's house. We were a little early, and so was everyone else. I didn't know Mrs. Halpin had so many students. Mrs. Halpin answered the door. We stepped into the living room. It was full of people, mostly mothers and little girls. They were all chatting and eating little cakes. I didn't know anyone, and all of a sudden I was worried. My mother chatted briefly with Mrs. Halpin and some other mother, and we took our seats, Mom in a big stuffed easy chair, me sitting on the edge of the same chair.

Mrs. Halpin stepped to the center of the living room, and the room hushed. "Thank you all so much for coming. I know how hard these boys and girls have worked, and I'm sure you will all enjoy their performances. And so without further ado..." She kept talking and introduced someone. I didn't hear who it was. My head was spinning. I was trying to figure out how to get out of there. What was I doing there? I didn't know my music. I didn't work hard. *Please God kill me now*, I prayed. Then I listened.

A little girl had gone to the beautiful baby grand Steinway in the far corner of the crowded living room. She was already playing. She was playing my song, *Swans on the Lake*. I held my breath. *Please God, make her be terrible*. That prayer was not to be answered. She glided through the piece effortlessly; almost perfect. I hated her. When she finished, sincere polite applause bubbled up in the room.

It'll Be Okay In The Morning

"Thank you, Margaret, that was lovely," sang Mrs. Halpin. I wondered. *Who was next? How much time do I have? Maybe I can make myself sick and throw up right here in Mom's lap. Maybe I'll die then she'll be sorry she made me take those stupid lessons. Yeah, this is all her fault. Her and that fat Mrs. Halpin.*

Someone else was playing, but I really couldn't hear, couldn't think. Then someone else played, but it was all just background noise until I heard. "Brian Cosacchi." Oh my God, that's me. I wanted to yell, "I'm not ready." My head was spinning. I slipped off the edge of the chair. Mom handed me my music as if that would make any difference. I trudged to the piano in a fog. I saw Mrs. Halpin's face smiling at me from somewhere. The piano's big white teeth were bared and smiling at me. The smile said, " You should have practiced. I'm going to eat you now." Its mouth opened wide to swallow me as I sat down. The piano was laughing, and it grabbed my legs. I couldn't move. The room was spinning. I balanced my music on the piano's upper lip and began to play. I knew the first part. I didn't need the music for that. I didn't need it for the rest of it either because I couldn't read it anyway.

I came to the end of the part I knew and I just kept going. *Not bad,* I thought. *They'll never know.* And I just kept playing; black keys, white keys, a little up here, a little down there. But it started to go bad, and I didn't know how to end it. I glanced up from the piano. Ms Halpin was looking back, glaring in disapproval. I just burst into tears and bolted from the piano in front of all those kids and mothers. I ran to my mother and buried my face in her lap and cried. When it was over Ms Halpin served cake to everyone. I didn't have any. And I didn't have to take any more piano lessons.

Chapter 20.
Dr. Finelli

From the time I was six or seven, we went to see him twice a year, and after the first year or two I tried to hide or get sick rather than make the trip. His office was on the third floor of a four story brick building in Mamaroneck, New York. We took the elevator, and as the doors opened I smelled the sweet medicinal odor of cloves mixed with something like wintergreen. It was a powerful smell. I think it was to cover the stink of rotting dead bodies hidden behind the walls—victims of Dr. Finelli. Anyway, the smell filled the beige ceramic-walled hallway and always made me more anxious. We arrived at the office door. The milky white glass window had his name stenciled on it: Dr. David Finelli, DDS.

Arriving for the visit to Dr. Finelli was filled with terrible anticipation and an air of hope that this year Dr. Finelli wouldn't find any cavities. I don't recall that ever happening, but it was always a hope. More realistic was the possibility of only one or two cavities and maybe just one terrible, torturous civilized session. It all depended on whether God thought I had been very bad or just bad.

We entered the stark waiting room, hard backed chairs and a hard looking, hard feeling leather couch. I chastised myself: "You'll be sorry you ate all that candy. You'll be sorry you didn't brush every day." The doctor's assistant greeted us pleasantly enough, "Please have a seat. Dr. Finelli will be with you in just a few minutes." We waited. I made myself think of other things, anything; our fort on the hill, basketball, football. But the present kept pushing its way through the good stuff, *Yeah, it's going to hurt. He always finds cavities. He likes to hurt people.*

Dr. Finelli appeared, smiling off-handedly. He had dark hair, with a pencil thin mustache. He looked like Don Amice. He wore a white official dentist's jacket that buttoned from the shoulder to the collarbone.

"Come on in, Brian," he'd say, leading the way into the soundproof torture chamber where all the dead kids were buried in the walls. He looked back over his shoulder at Mom in a knowing way as if to reassure her, "Don't worry if you hear a little screaming, Kathleen, he'll be fine." I screwed up my courage, entered the pit. The dental chair yawned and stretched, and I mounted it.

"Well, let's see how we've been doing, shall we? Let's have a look. Open wide," he said as if we were doing it together. He adjusted the big spotlight that floated in front of me, pulling and pushing until it was just right and he could see all the way down into my stomach. I began sweating.

He thoughtfully considered a vast collection of silver torture hooks left over from the Inquisition. These were all laid out neatly, antiseptically, on a white cloth that covered a fluted glass tray. The skinniest hooks with points so fine they seemed to disappear were the most fearful. He picked one and began sticking its almost invisible tip between my teeth one at a time, searching, digging. Sooner or later the sharp pointed tip stopped, stuck—hung up on some crack or the tiniest of holes. My body braced like a steel bar in anticipation of his next move. I knew he would go exploring, twisting, churning that sadist's spear around until he hit a sweet spot; a spot that caused such a shock when he found it that my entire body would lift from the chair. But Dr. Finelli would just begin humming something, turn away for a moment and make a mark on a chart. Then he returned and continued poking and pulling and digging until he had found every crack and crevice that needed to be fixed—to be drilled and filled. Then I had to come back and bear the unbearable. I endured Dr. Finelli's house of pain by shutting out and rationalizing. I didn't think about my next visit, didn't worry about the picks and the drills until the moment was upon me and then, until this one day, I obediently complied, telling myself, *There's no way out*, and *All the other kids have to do it*.

But on this one black day, when I thought of Dr. Finelli looming over me with picks and drills, I rebelled. I wasn't going back to Dr. Finelli and his picks and drills! I told Mom, "NO, I'm not going." Mom was aghast. She didn't know what to do. So she did what she always did when she didn't know what to do. She called Dad. I heard him screaming on the other end of the phone. The fat was in the fire now! No turning back! I knew I would lose this battle, but I would fight.

I sat on the stairs leading from the hallway to the upstairs bedroom while Mom pleaded for Dad to control himself, but instead Dad turned up the decibels. He was coming home. As usual, almost before Mom hung up the phone, the 1949 Kaiser pulled up in front of the house. Dad had set another record for the mile or so from the Spencer Pharmacy to our front door.

I was still sitting on the stairs, my hands holding the banister spindles when he charged into the house. The Venetian blind on the glass door between the sun porch and the outside world clattered several times back and forth as Dad slammed it behind him. He glared up at me and in a controlled but on-the-verge voice, while biting his lower lip, he said, "Now whasis your mopher tells fe agout your refusing to go and get your teeph fixed." I didn't respond. He continued, "Do you rearize I had to croze the store, leaf my cussomers to come here." It wasn't a question. "Do you reary ant to grow up and have no teeph in your head like Raspberry?" He continued as he marched up the staircase, "It costs me good money to send you to the dentist and, so help me God, you're going." I clung to the spindles. Dad grabbed my legs. I yelled, "Nooooo," and held on with all my might. Dad pulled harder to no avail. My body rose up off the stairs, secured on one end by Dad pulling, lifting my legs and on the other by me desperately grasping the spindles. But the stalemate ended. Dad gave up pulling my legs. He peeled my fingers from the spindles and said nothing—just continued to bite his lower lip. I conceded. Dad, not Mom, would take me to the dentist this day.

We drove the 5 miles to Mamaroneck without a sound except my sniffling. Once again I walked the green mile to the clove-smelling office. Dr. Finelli appeared. "Pete, what are you doing here? Good to see you. How are you, Brian? Ready? Let's see what we can finish today." Dad rose and approached Dr. Finelli. They had a brief mumbled conversation and turned toward me. "Come on in, Brian. Your Dad and I want to talk to you." My heart rose to my throat and began to pound. I floated into the office, and Dr. Finelli began, "Your Dad thinks it might be good to try some Novocain on you. What do you think?" It was a question. I thought, *Cane, Nova cane, hurricane, sugar cane, what the heck is Nova cane?*

He went on, "Your Dad thinks that if we give you some Novocain it will help relieve some of the discomfort. Would you like that?"

Relieve the discomfort! Would I like that? Would I? What's the catch? Why didn't I get this cane thing before?

It'll Be Okay In The Morning

What do I have to do to get it? My head spun. I couldn't think. I think I said yes, and I mounted the rack. The light was blinding, my head was spinning. Dr. Finelli had his back to me for a moment. Then he turned and there in his right hand, held high, its tip leaking a drop or two of ooze, was the longest needle I had ever seen. I wanted to ask, "What are you going to do with that?" But I couldn't, and I already knew anyway.

"Finelli the Frightful" simply said, "Open." I complied. The hand moved toward my mouth, but long before it arrived the oozing silver tip began to find its way into my mouth, my jaw, deeper and deeper. He twisted and swiveled, and dug the pinpoint deeper and deeper. He started pressing the plunger. I could see his thumb pushing. I could feel my jaw filling with the cane stuff. I thought the needle would come out my cheek somewhere near my chin. My jaw was exploding. I was talking to myself through the pain. *This will be worthwhile. Oh yes! The drilling won't hurt anymore. EEEOOOWWWW, I'll take the drilling. Stop the needle!*

Too late. What seemed like an hour had been seconds. But it would be worth it, I told myself—I kept telling myself. I breathed again for the first time since the hand moved into my mouth. Finelli the Fearful said, "We'll wait a minute or two to let the Novocain work."

We waited. I was sweating. I rested, waiting for round two, believing the discomfort would be relieved. The minutes flew, and the Frightful returned to his fiendish mission.

The dentist's drill in those olden days was a simple belt-driven arrangement. Not the high speed, high tech, quick, in and out, drills of the past 30 or 40 years. These were grinders. The bit of the drill turned so slowly that occasionally it would catch and stop and pull and twist my jaw and my head along with it. The vibrations were so strong it felt like a jackhammer rattling my head back and forth. The sound was so loud bouncing off all the bone in my head and jaw it was like someone yelling at me at the top of their lungs. Sometimes I talked to the drill—carried on a conversation—*Hey, drill I promise I'll be good. Please don't hurt me too much today.* It never listened—just laughed in that jackhammer mocking voice.

The promise of discomfort relief on this day was not to be. The Novocain flunked the test. The Frightful Finelli bored in with his trusty grinder. The grinder always knew exactly where to find the nerve of the tooth, like radar. It took a little time for it to find the most tender, most vulnerable, delicate pain responsive spot. And I always knew when he was getting close as the drill head played around the edges of that sad spot, toying, teasing before striking and landing with supernatural ferocity. The pain it evoked was sublime, pure, and so complete as to leave scars on my soul so deep that I can still feel that drill sixty years later.

Chapter 21.
Elementary School

A six-year-old star in first grade…that was me. And at seven and eight and nine. All my teachers at Halstead Avenue School, Miss Shea, Miss Phillips, the first Miss Devlin, Miss Kiernan, Miss Marinon loved me. I was polite and a little impish. (Haven't really changed much in 60 years.) Each year the contest for top honors in my class was between Arthur Klein and me. Arthur's father was the Superintendent of Schools. A lot was expected of Arthur. Not so much of me.

Even though I was the second smallest kid in my class—maybe an inch taller then Mark Biseglia—I loved sports and was pretty good at most despite my size. In those days we played knock-out in gym. It's now called dodge-ball. In those days there wasn't the concern for injury that exists today. We didn't wear helmets or protective gear, and no one was ever injured beyond a brief time out for a few tears.

Everyone was afraid of Big Frank Solazzo. He was "Big Frank." Even at eight he towered almost a full head above the second tallest kid in the class, and he was solid as a rock. In knock-out he threw the volleyball-sized ball by curling it into the crook of his arm and hurling it at frightened opponents. Very few kids tried to catch the ball. Most chose to retreat, jump around or hide behind a fellow teammate. Big Frank's overall knock-out record was impressive, but there were a couple of us that Big Frank had trouble knocking out. We could catch Big Frank's power throw. It frustrated the big guy that a twerp like me could knock him out. I can't say I always caught it, but it was enough times to earn Big Frank's respect.

We played sand lot football; nothing organized. We just got together after school or on Saturdays, chose up sides and played. The only protective gear anyone had was a helmet, and even those were rare. I finally got a helmet when I was ten. What a treat. I loved that helmet. I loved the way it looked, the way it felt, even the way it smelled. That helmet made a new person of me. I loved to carry the ball. All kids do. But even as small as I was, I was really good at it and could drag three or four kids along with me on my back for a good distance. Now with my new helmet I had a new weapon, and I became the "Power Peanut," head down, plowing straight ahead. I earned the nicknames "Torpedo" and "Mighty Mouse" from my peers. These very young years were the only ones I could feel good about for a long, long time—for another ten years.

Something happened in fifth grade—in the second Miss Devlin's class. All of sudden I began to get stupid and not care. I'd like to blame it on the nightmare at home. I'd like to think that that the hopelessness I felt at ten made me give up for the next ten years. But it is just as likely that no one cared how I was doing, and so I just decided not to do anything.

My handwriting was terrible. I sat in class with comic books opened inside my social studies book. I didn't get fractions and didn't ask for help. In general, I bombed out.

The first time I was sent to the principal's office I was frightened, but after the fifth or sixth time with no negative consequences, I wasn't frightened anymore. Miss Devlin's frustration with me showed. She thought I could do better and told me so time and time again.

The end of the school year came and I was just getting by, doing as little as absolutely required. We had begun our study of Civics. We spent some time learning about our justice system—judges, juries, attorneys. And as an example of how it worked Miss Devlin decided to have a mock trial. She chose me as the defendant. My lawyer was Roseanne Germano, a very smart but quiet little girl, and the prosecuting attorney was my best friend, Leonard, "Chi Chi Beans" Galliulo. Miss Devlin was the judge. I was accused of loafing, disrupting the class and not doing my best. The rest of the class was the jury.

This didn't seem like a mock trial. To me it was a real! Roseanne was not a good attorney and, as I recall, did more to convict me than acquit me. But then my very good friend "Chi Chi Beans" stood before the class and excoriated me, roasted me, burned me. He was a ten-year-old William Jennings Bryan, an orator equal to Demosthenes. *This is my good friend?* I kept asking myself. I didn't have a chance. And as the judge instructed the jury, I was escorted to the "jail"—the cloakroom at the back of the class. It had heavy wooden bi-fold doors, and there was little room inside. I squeezed myself in and sat down. The jury deliberated. I waited, half happy that I was a star again, a little afraid of what the punishment would be if found guilty.

It didn't take long, just a few minutes. The doors opened, and Big Frank and John Matero escorted me back to my desk. Miss Devlin wasted no time. "How does the jury find?" she asked. Ann Ortiz rose and read the verdict. "We find the defendant guilty, your honor." I felt relieved. Miss Devlin looked at me, almost smiled and said: "Brian Cosacchi, having been found guilty of the charges against you, you are hereby sentenced to spend one year in Mrs. McGowan's sixth grade. The jury is excused."

Chapter 22.
Last Years of Elementary School— 6th Grade

Having been expelled from Miss Devlin's 5th grade, I moved on to the 6th grade. Mrs. McGowan was our homeroom teacher and our math teacher. She was no nonsense, and when I picked up where I left off—doing nothing—she sent me to the office of Mr. Marshall, the principal. For me, school was a distraction from life's purpose, surviving and watching TV. I still liked sports and spent time pretending to be Bob Cousy shooting baskets by myself against the backboard we erected on the light pole on the corner. But even interest in sports was diminishing, and I sank into a solitary fantasyland.

It was 1951, and television was still new. I watched almost anything and drifted off into my own Never Never Land. Pretend became survival. I loved all the little kids stuff, Rootie Kazootie, Tom Corbet, Space Cadet and Sky King. Now in 6th grade, I graduated to more grown up entertainment like Mr. Wizard and a very soft-spoken artist named John Nagy.

John Nagy taught people to draw things they never would have been able to without his help. And he was so nice, calm, quiet. You could hear his breathing as he sketched and instructed his TV audience. He was soothing. I loved John Nagy. He made me believe I could draw and one day be a famous artist. So I practiced all the time, even in Miss McGowan's math class. I didn't understand the math anyway so I thought I might as well devote my life to art. Mrs. McGowan decided she would become a collector of my art after each class, and she shared my artistic expression with Mr. Marshall.

My collection became so extensive that Mr. Marshall decided that my work should not be kept a secret any more, and he invited my parents in to discuss my future. We all gathered in his office, and out came some of my more recent work. My mother gasped. My father's mouth dropped. *What can they be looking at?* I wondered, *Is it that good?*

Then they showed me. It was a picture that John Nagy had taught me to draw. It was a picture of an elephant from the rear looking back over his shoulder. It wasn't exactly Picasso so I knew they would not be sending me off to art school right away, but I also saw nothing so outrageous about my elephant other than the fact that I drew it during one of Mrs. McGowan's math classes. I was sent back to my class, and Mr. Marshall conferred with Mom and Dad. Nothing really changed.

It wasn't until years later that my mother told me that their chagrin was caused by their interpretation of my art. My elephant had his back turned to the observer. His tail therefore, was prominent in the drawing. But neither Mom nor Dad nor Mr. Marshall nor Mrs. McGowan saw a tail. They all saw a "butt crack" and thought I was drawing a dirty picture. Even without knowing this at the time, it was clear to me that my innate artistic talent and chosen career had come to a crashing halt. Somehow I got through sixth and seventh grade and was promoted "on condition" to eighth grade—Junior High School.

"On condition" was formal probation. I either shaped up and cut it or went backwards. I was afraid and struggled to change. It was almost too late.

Chapter 23.
Aunt Angelina's

When we were children, Dad's family was always generous to us at Christmas and Easter. I don't think we ever thanked them properly. We just didn't know any better. It wasn't expected.

And on those special holidays we set out for the big house on Ellsworth Street In Rye—-the house where the Italian clan lived—- the "house of Anthonys." I thought of it that way because it seemed to me almost everyone there was Anthony.

There was Grandpa Anthony Cosacchi and his brother-in-law Anthony Santoro (who married Grandpa's sister Angelina) and his son Anthony and his son's son Anthony. Then there was my Uncle Joe's son—my cousin—Anthony Cosacchi and my Cousin Tina's son Anthony Carella. And of course I'm part Anthony, Dad settling for it as my middle name. I never liked the name Anthony. It wasn't very special. I'm glad my Mom held out for Brian. It's a fine gift she gave me.

Great Great Grandma, Dad's Grandmother, waited inside the front door to greet us. She was in her nineties. She looked as though she was in her hundreds; stooped and smiling, deep creases etched her face. She didn't know a word of English except "Nice-a, nice-a" spoken through a mouth of many missing teeth and always accompanied by a surprisingly strong pinch on the cheek.

The house was large and clean and Italian, brown stucco walls outside, beige stucco walls inside. It smelled of the sweet and pungent remnants of thousands of wonderful meals cooked over the years in the big kitchen. Everything in the house looked old to me, even if it was new. The living room was dark and formal and uncomfortable looking with dark-colored overstuffed furniture and lace doilies tactfully placed on their backs and arms. Old fashioned floor lamps hung over winged easy chairs. Translucent brown and beige shades with little fuzzy balls hanging from their perimeter muted the light so as to make everything in the room look even older. A bronze sculpture of a naked woman reclining on a rock and holding up an amber-colored light held a place of prominence on the heavy wooden coffee table.

For us kids spending the entire afternoon at Aunt Angelina's would have been excruciating; nothing much to do except listen to old people speaking Italian, arguing and agreeing, fighting and loving—mostly loving I think. But never sure what was going on. It was all filled with passion, hugs and kisses and laughs and tears; people rushing about in the kitchen or dozing off in the overstuffed furniture.

What made the days wonderful and so memorable were the feasts created by the team of "old lady chefs" led by Aunt Angelina and assisted by Aunts Minnie, Florence, Gina and Lois.

When we were called to table, we knew we would be sitting for a couple of hours. The table filled the dinning room; the tail end extended into the living room where we children sat. Everyone had their pecking order place with Grandpa Cosacchi at the head of the table out of deference to his position as head of the family. I never did understand that respect.

It'll Be Okay In The Morning

Grandpa's homemade red wine was poured for everyone. Even we children got a splash in our jelly glasses.

And then the courses started flowing from the kitchen.

For openers Aunt Angelina's Italian egg drop soup along with a marvelous antipasto, olives and salami and hard boiled eggs and anchovies over some kind of greens—maybe arugula or hearts of palm. I never ate the greens.

Then the good stuff: lasagna or mostaccioli with meat balls and sausage followed by tender juicy chicken pieces slowly baked in olive oil and seasoned with oregano and basil. Then braciole, thin slices of beef rolled as a roulade with cheese and bread crumbs and fried in its own juices—mmmmmmm.

The feast continued with Angelina's specialties: artichokes stuffed with breadcrumbs, garlic and tons of Parmesan cheese slowly steamed to mix all the flavors and melt cheese.

But for me, the best was one of the last, Aunt Angelina's suplee, a rice croquette stuffed with mozzarella cheese and deep fried so the cheese melted and transformed the rice into something special—something totally different—a taste never to be forgotten. I could eat a hundred.

Then *dolce*, dessert—sweet, marvelous Italian pastry, cannoli, angels (custard stuffed sponge cake shaped like angels), ricotta pie, rum baba, apple torte, along with biscuit tortoni and spumoni ice cream.

Finally, to help digest all that had gone before, a magnificent fruit bowl with wonderful things I have rarely seen outside of Great Grandma's home; red oranges, grapes the size of golf balls and prickly pears. The fruit bowl was accompanied by a bowl of nuts in the shell along with little cups of powerful espresso and maybe a little brandy or anisette.

We never made it to the nuts, espresso and anisette. We went outside to play while all the overstuffed old people stretched out on all the overstuffed furniture and snoozed.

I smile when I think about those wonderful feasts.

God bless you, Aunt Angelina, and I'm sorry for never thanking you properly.

Chapter 24.
Darkness: The Attic and the Cellar

I didn't know what it meant when Dad began to sleep with me and Bruce in our bedroom. We didn't mind. We had room. I was just four or five. Sheila was recently born. But it signaled the beginning of the awful change that took place in our family—sickness that ruined our spirit. It didn't take long—just a few years.

If I had known then what clinical depression was—if I had understood alcoholism—I might have forgiven my mother—I might not have tried so hard to "fix" her. I didn't know, and I never could forgive her. Not even now, God rest her soul.

It may not have been the first episode in the nightmare, but it was near the beginning and it is the most remembered. That day Bruce and I got home from school early. I was probably eight or nine. We walked home as usual. It was only a half-mile to Halstead Avenue School. Mom was always home doing laundry in the basement, listening to one of the afternoon soap operas, working in the garden or trying to cook. She was always home. But today she wasn't there. We hollered, "Mom, we're home!" She didn't answer. We decided to change and go out to play. Upstairs we charged. I got a head start, "Last one up is a rotten egg," I yelled. And Bruce replied "Yeah, and the first one eats it."

As we put on our after school clothes, we kept hearing a barely audible bumping noise. It was coming from outside or somewhere upstairs in the attic. Then a second sound joined the soft bumping, like someone humming. The noises gave me an uncomfortable, scary feeling, like being alone in the house at night in the dark. "Lets look upstairs," we silently agreed, although neither of us wanted to.

The door to the attic was in the short hallway between the two larger bedrooms. The door was always stuck closed but now it was ajar. We opened the door to the narrow, shallow, four-foot square entrance. A flight of free-standing wooden steps went up at an almost 90 degree angel. Two of us could not fit in the entrance together. I started up first. I could only see straight up like being at the bottom of a well. I heard the noise—the soft bumping noise. The humming sound changed and now sounded more like growling, and I was very frightened. I let Bruce go up the steps ahead of me.

He climbed up hand over hand with me close behind. When he got close to the top he could see over the edge. He yelled. He yelled louder than anyone had ever yelled "Mom, Mom, Mom!" I felt dizzy and sick to my stomach. What was up there? I didn't want to think, but horrible pictures popped into my head. I couldn't see. I was looking straight up at Bruce's backside. Then he climbed onto the attic floor. I hurried after him. When I got to the top I saw too. Bruce continued to yell "Mom, Mom!" She was there, close to the edge of the stairwell, standing tippy toe on an orange crate holding on for dear life to a rope she had fixed to the rafter above and tied around her neck. She was choking. The crate was wobbling, making that soft muffled noise as it bumped back and forth, side to side. Mom couldn't talk. She moaned and gurgled, choking. I realized I was yelling, too "Mom, Mom, Mom! Why? What are you doing?"

It'll Be Okay In The Morning

In an instant my big brother became my much older brother. "Hold her legs up Bri." And he scrambled back down the stairs returning just a moment later with the big kitchen knife. He climbed up on the big trunk next to where Mom was teetering and cut the rope. Mom collapsed with a sigh on top of me and gently fell to the attic floor.

I don't recall if she said anything. I rocked back and forth crying, uncontrolled sobs that just poured from my throat. "Mom, Mom! Why? What are you doing?" The terrors had begun.

To this day I don't know if Mom was just trying to scare us. Who wants to believe their mother is capable of such sadism? But for all the years to come we would hold our breaths waiting for the next surprise from Mom. There were dozens. We never got used to them. Whenever we couldn't find her, a dark, desperate feeling swept over us. We grew up wishing someone else's—anyone else's mom was our mom.

Chapter 25.
Hide and Go Seek

On one late crisp autumn afternoon I returned from playing some after-school football. I went upstairs to change. In those days a weekly bath was the norm unless you smelled like road kill. As I changed, I was very aware that I had not seen or heard Mom. I didn't want to think about it. I can't remember where Bruce and Sheila were.

It was dark now, getting close to dinnertime. No sign of Mom. I began to feel an empty, sick feeling, for no matter how lousy a cook my mother was, except for the nights of drunken stupor, she was always there at this hour to burn or boil something into submission. Bruce and Sheila were now there, and we all worried. Dad was never home for dinner during the week, finding his escape in the store. We were alone.

With great trepidation we began our search, barely, quietly calling, "Mommm." To get past the worst possibility, we took a flashlight and checked the attic. We didn't bother calling. We resolutely opened the attic door, which we noted with optimism hadn't been left ajar. The stream of light from the flashlight was comforting as Bruce checked the up stairs. No Mom! Still, where was she? It was well past dinnertime. Something was definitely wrong. We reluctantly continued our search of the house. The only place we hadn't looked was the cellar. Our cellar was a very scary place. We mustered our courage.

Brian Cosacchi

The wood paneled cellar was always dark and damp and cold even in summer. It smelled like wet chalk. The ceilings were dropped with recessed fluorescent fixtures that didn't give much light. Anyone over 5'10" would have to be careful not to bump their head. The knotty pine paneling was built out from the original stone walls, leaving a three-foot gap for storage. The storage area was accessed by a couple of doors made from the same wood paneling.

We turned on the one light that illuminated the cellar stairs and descended with our flashlight. Not a sound. At the bottom Bruce reached up and pulled the chain on the first fluorescent. Again we were relieved to see no Mom. The fear returned. If not here, where? To the left was the laundry room; no door, very dark and no illumination. The furnace was in there. I held my breath, turned on the flashlight and slowly, squinting through half closed eyes that didn't want to see, scanned the inside. No Mom.

One more place to look. At the far end of the cellar, around the corner, was the door to the coal cellar, a little room that stored our coal in those days before oil heat. The room was under our little back porch, cold with no light. If she wasn't here, she must have gone out somewhere. I opened the door that separated the cellar from the coal cellar. I shined the flashlight to the back of the little stone room and saw no mother, dead or alive. I was relieved.

Bruce had already turned to go back upstairs when I remembered the space between the knotty pine and cellar wall. No way! Couldn't be! But, just to be sure, I lifted the little latch that kept the door closed and opened it. I choked off my breath, gasped "Oh my God!" Mom was sitting comfortably, squatting, perfectly still, expressionless in the cramped darkness on some old broken bookcases that had been stored there. "Leave me alone," she slurred.

"Bruce, Mom's here!" I yelled, and in the same breath, "Mom, what are you doing, why are you doing this?" I was frightened, sick—too frightened to cry. My head pounded. I cried.

I don't remember what happened after finding her there, how we got her back upstairs, what we told Dad, what happened that night, the next day. I don't remember how long it was before our next search for the missing Mom. I don't remember what happened after finding her, this next time in the coal cellar hiding in the dark; another frightening apparition for a ten-year old. I'd never get used to it.

Our troubles lasted for the rest of Mom's life. There were loud fights with flying pots and pans. At night the screaming and hollering and threats of murder from both sides woke us regularly. I cried and begged them to stop. They never would. So, I made up a ritual that helped me believe I controlled the madness. I decided that I had to be the last one to go to sleep at night so that everything would be okay in the morning. I stayed awake night after night for I don't know how long. (I still do.) It seemed to work. Things were always better in the morning.

On Sunday afternoons we had a big dinner at midday. Dad sacrificed and came home for his one afternoon with the family. It was usually a good day, and we would hope and pray that Mom would stay sober and Dad would keep his temper. Sometimes they didn't, and a conflagration would erupt. Sometimes I ran outside and hid behind the hedges or under the big willow.

One Sunday things went especially bad. Mom had been drinking. I could always tell. Her walk would turn to a shuffle, and she would continuously dart her tongue from her mouth to lick her upper lip. I always knew and could anticipate the violent, frightening consequences. On this Sunday, Mom made it through dinner. Then the arguing began. Dad was preparing to leave. But Mom wanted the last word. He was about to exit via the glass door to the sun porch when Mom hurled a pot from the kitchen. It missed and crashed against the door. Dad bit his upper lip in that angry imitation of a bulldog and returned to the kitchen. Mom had reloaded with some utensil or other, and Dad attempted to disarm her. She became hysterical, shuffling, screaming from the kitchen into the dining room. Dad pursued her and caught up to her near the day bed that was Mom's nap place. They tussled, Mom screaming and Dad yelling. Mom fell or was pushed to the bed and struggled kicking and screaming. Her right leg convulsed upwards and crashed through the glass storm window. Her hysterical screams drowned out the crying of her three children. Dad went to the phone and called Mr. O'Donnell from down the street. He asked him to please come and help. He was there in five minutes. Next Dad called Dr. Breiter, our family doctor and a friend to Dad. He arrived shortly and gave Mom a sedative. She calmed down, went to sleep and life returned to normal, miserable normal.

Dad tried to stop Mom's drinking. He made unannounced visits home. He searched. He drove up and down the main drag that went from Harrison to Rye, Mamaroneck, Larchmont and New Rochelle asking every liquor store owner on the route to please not sell to her. She continued to drink heavily.

I appointed myself the family sleuth tracking down the booze wherever she would hide it: quart bottles, pints, half pints, 16-ounce tumbler glasses filled with Carstairs hidden in every conceivable corner, coat closet, bureau drawer, bottom of the garbage pail, toilet tank, laundry room, storage areas, too many places. I couldn't find all of them all the time. Some days Mom would drink and then go to bed and sleep. I searched her room one day while she slept and uncovered a full 16-ounce tumbler hidden beneath some under garments in her top dresser drawer. I woke her, confronted her with the glass and told her she could have the booze or she could have me as her son. She reached up, slapped my face and took the tumbler. I didn't understand.

In time alcohol took it's toll. Over the next decade Mom tried or pretended suicide at least twice more; once with an overdose of pills and once dragged from the gas oven by Sheila. Poor Sheila! She bore the brunt of the darkness after Bruce and I went off to college. It drove her to the convent, and then she admitted herself, for just a brief time, to a mental hospital. She quickly realized she was saner than most people. She was just carrying too heavy a load.

After 15 years Mom's liver began to go. If she kept drinking, she would die of cirrhosis. But she lived to be 80. She stopped needing the booze. She was the wife of a pharmacist who prescribed and dispensed effective, illegal substitutes for relief from whatever tortured her. In effect she became an addict in place of a drunk.

For me, after fourth grade, living in the house at #3 Second Street was a day-to-day question that I tried not to think about. Thank God my life was filled up with lots of other things that kept me out of the house most of the time; pick up games of any sport, alone adventures with my dog Tippy into the Cosacchi Mountains and the woods on West Street, Boy Scouts every Wednesday night, altar boys, helping Dad at the store. There wasn't too much time to be with Mom, but each day I held my breath hoping she would be okay. I prayed a lot. God was my friend, and I thought he wanted me to worry as hard as I could. I thought if I worried hard enough for all my sins, everything would turn out all right. The worrying didn't do any real good, but I felt I was doing something. Those were difficult years. It seemed to me even the weather changed, more floods, colder winters.

Just to add to the pebble pile, for a while the house was infested with rats. I could hear them scratching and scraping in my bedroom walls at night. They sounded as though they were coming right through the walls, and every night for about a year I expected them to. Dad said they were just squirrels. But one night our little dog, Tippy, took one on in the basement. It was half as big as Tippy. Tippy prevailed and left no doubt we had rats. Dad finally had to admit it, and in a few days the exterminator had them all gone. As scary as they were, the rats had been an almost welcome distraction from the rest of life at # 3 Second Street—and we abided.

Chapter 26.
On to High School

Since sixth grade I had become a loner. I was embarrassed and humiliated by my mother and by my own failings. Entering eighth grade on probation was only a little wake-up call, and I made only a little effort. I didn't feel I belonged anywhere any more; no friends, no activities, just the TV and food. I was plodding out of latency into adolescence looking for encouragement and caring.

I didn't do well enough in eighth grade. I fell short of "acceptable," and Dad decided I needed a stricter school—a Catholic school—the school my brother was attending. Of course! One more time I was to follow my successful brother. I was the only one from Harrison to enter Archbishop Stepinac High School in 1954. No matter, I had no friends anyway. Bruce and I had to take a bus from Harrison to Mamaroneck, then change buses there to get to White Plains. The trip each morning took about an hour for the fifteen miles.

I didn't know anyone in my class. They came from all over the Archdiocese, some from as far as Pawling forty miles away. I couldn't do anything well, so I wasn't "in" anything. I just went home each night, pretended to do homework, watched TV and ate. By the end of sophomore year I had eaten myself into a whopping 5'3" 193 pounds of worthless nerd.

I watched Bruce's successes with admiration and jealousy. He started his own dance band and appeared on television on the old Ted Mack Amateur Hour. I was proud of him. He was the drum major for the marching band, and he had lots of girlfriends. He did well academically.

I didn't do anything but wish. I got into mischief a lot. I set a record for detention in sophomore year for accidentally hitting Father Sullivan, The Dean of Discipline, in the head with a snowball.

Things were not going well.

I was the little fat nerd, picked on and bullied.

Sophomore year math was geometry. Everyone had sharp pointed compasses. Just for fun Dick Flintoff jabbed me in the butt. I laughed a little but it hurt a lot and soon became infected. After a few weeks of trying to deal with the growing abscess alone, too embarrassed to say anything to anyone, it became impossible to bear, and I wound up in the hospital to have the fistula painfully cut out.

A few months later, sitting by myself at lunch, one of the big dumb football players, John Shea, stepped up beside me, laughing his big dumb laugh. He semi-shouted to his admiring friends, "Hey kid, you want a fix?" and jabbed the sharp point of the compass so deep into my arm that it bled right through the lining of my sport coat. I couldn't stand it. And as he turned to walk away still laughing, I launched my 193 pound flabby frame at him hitting him full force at about waist high. Big John reacted a bit startled as if he had been jostled getting into a subway. Then he realized what had happened—who it was—and flicked me off like a small bit of bird dropping. He and his friends just continued and laughed some more.

It'll Be Okay In The Morning

I reported the incident. I didn't care if it made me a "marked man." I would have justice. There was a conference with Shea's parents, Father Sullivan, the Dean of Discipline, and Monsignor Krug. There was no one to represent me. Big John was only suspended for a few days. After all, he was the star football player, and I was just a fat nerd. John eventually ran for school president. What a travesty it would have been if he had won.

Life was miserable as a fat, dumb nerd. To add to the misery, Dad made me join the band. He thought I could just pick up the clarinet where I had left off several years before, which was nowhere. He thought Bruce's example, playing lead trumpet, would be an inspiration. It wasn't. I couldn't read music very well and squeaked and squeaked so much that the lead clarinet sitting in front of me turned around and said something very disparaging and pinched me so hard I almost started to cry.

I didn't make it as a clarinet player, so Father McGann put me in percussion playing the cymbals, but I had trouble counting measures. People playing percussion spend most of their time waiting for their big moment to hit the drum, shake the tambourine, ring the bell, crash the cymbals. While they usually get a cue from the conductor, it is their responsibility to keep track of where they are by counting the measures, 1234, 1234, twenty, thirty, forty or more times.

I wasn't good at counting measures and choked more often than not. And so, at our spring concert, the orchestra played one of the beautiful pavanes. Almost at the very end of the piece there was to be a single cymbal crash. The other guys in the percussion knew I wasn't good at counting measures and decided to have some fun at my expense. So, long before the proper moment—in the middle of the most beautiful, somber, peaceful part of the piece, Ray

Deluca whispered, "Are you ready? Better get ready. Here it comes. It's the next measure." I panicked, grabbed my cymbals, 1-2-3- crash! Ooops! Father McGann nearly fell off the podium. He jutted his neck out, snapped his teeth together, clenched his eyes shut and winced painfully. The baton that had been moving in a rhythmic up, down, out, and back, came to an abrupt stop in mid air and trembled in his right hand. It only took a second for him to regain his composure.

I quit the band. Father McGann was relieved. And so it went for three miserable years until I just had to do something. I could no longer live that way.

As junior year came to a close, and with me hanging on by only a thread both at home and at school, I decided to change. I wasn't going to be a fat nerd anymore!

Even more than my academic and athletic failures, I was getting frantic about my social disaster. I was almost seventeen, and hormones were flowing. I had watched my brother dating Ginny Yans and Renee Brulatour and other pretty girls before going off to Notre Dame. I heard guys in my class talking about their girlfriends. I saw the girls from Good Counsel Academy and Our Lady Of Victory coming to Stepinac for chorus and theatre and sporting events, flirting and cavorting. I hated myself.

Chapter 27.
The Kiss

I was almost seventeen and had never held a girls' hand, let alone been kissed. Not even one of those cute, totally innocent things that neighborhood kids do when they're growing up. The only "encounter" with the opposite sex I had was with Roseanne Quinn when we showed each other our special parts when we were seven.

But here I was almost seventeen and had never been kissed. And the way my life was going, I never would be. Kissing a girl was number one on my wish list since the hormones began bubbling several years before. I dreamed of someday having a girlfriend who would let me kiss her. As a good Catholic teenager, and from what I could see of my mother and father, I believed that women didn't really like kissing or any of the other sexual things men did to women. But they reluctantly granted kisses and those other favors to attractive men if they were gentlemen and gave them things and took them places and spent a lot of money on them. They only liked attractive men, and I was just a fat little dwarf, Tweedle Dum, a court jester.

I was neither popular nor unpopular. I had neither friends nor enemies. No one noticed me at all. They didn't try to avoid me, they just had no reason to get to know someone so inconsequential, so inconspicuous. That's what I was, inconspicuous, inconsequential! No girl, let alone an attractive one, would ever waste their time with me. So, I dreamed. At night when I went to bed, in the secret darkness, I imagined. I propped my pillow in the crook of my arm, buried my face in it and pretended I was kissing a beautiful girl. Not just any girl. I thought, as long as I had to pretend, I might as well make her beautiful: Gina Lollobrigida, Sophia Loren, Brigitte Bardot. But now, at almost seventeen, I was tired of pretending. My pillow was no longer enough.

It was the summer of junior year, and I was tired of being the fat, roly-poly Tweedle Dum. I was going to change. I was going to lose weight and maybe, one day, get to kiss a girl. I asked Dad for help—some new pill that would help fat people lose weight. Dad refused, "It's just baby fat. You'll lose it when the time is right." The refusal cemented my resolve. I would lose that weight! I would get to 150 pounds and do it by Thanksgiving! I went on a starvation diet, and the pounds peeled off.

School started a few weeks later, and I lost the forty pounds long before the self imposed Thanksgiving deadline. I weighed 152 pounds. People didn't recognize me. I was still inconsequential, but I wasn't inconsequential *and* fat anymore. No more Tweedle Dum. For the first time in a long time I was proud. I would do better this year.

I got my driver's license and began to drive one of the two family cars to school, a blue 1954 Plymouth. I joined the high school chorus. We sang with the girls' chorus from Good Counsel Academy and practiced Wednesdays after school. I liked singing and loved being around girls even if they looked right through me. But I had changed more than I realized. The girls were looking. And on one of those practice Wednesdays, as I drove some friends onto the Good Counsel campus, I noticed several girls chatting. One of them, a very popular and attractive brunette, looked at the car, smiled brightly and waved. I knew she must be waving at someone else, Pat DeSena or John Colgan, and didn't give it a second thought except to wish she was waving and smiling at me.

The next day the Good Counsel girl's network went to work. So-and-So's girlfriend told her boyfriend to tell the boy driving the blue Plymouth that Kathy Crowley thought he was cute and wanted to go out with him. The message filtered through the system. I got the message and was terrified. *She must have meant someone else in the car—or some other blue Plymouth. This is just a bad joke people are playing on me. Maybe she doesn't see very well...She'll be disappointed. What do I tell her? What do I say? Where would I take her?*

Courage and desire prevailed, and I called her. My conversation was labored, stilted, awkward. Hers: friendly, fun, reassuring. We went to a movie and afterward to Daddy Michael's, a popular ice cream parlor. Several people greeted Kathy, but no one knew the guy she was with. Kathy was fun and beautiful and I relaxed a little. Conversation came easier. I didn't feel so dumb and boring. When we were finished, I drove her home.

Kathy lived in an apartment complex, so I parked the car in one of the designated spaces in front of her unit. We sat for a moment. She made no move to leave. Just enough light from outside painted her face. She was beautiful. Her eyes gleamed. She was smiling softly. I thought, *Is it possible? A girl this pretty? On a first date? Me?* She sat close to me. *Is she leaning toward me? Is she getting closer? She is!*

I tried to think of something to say. "Gee, Kathy thanks for coming." Was I about to make a complete fool of myself? Could this be the moment I dreamed of? She was so pretty. I leaned toward her slowly so as not to frighten her or make a fool of myself. I began to say something but she moved closer, and it happened. She didn't scream, laugh, or slap me. I didn't know who kissed who. It didn't matter. I didn't think at all anymore. There were explosions inside me. She wrapped her arms and hands around my neck and pulled me closer, kissing me harder. It felt the way I thought it should feel on my lips—on my mouth. But the surging in the rest of my body was unexpected, unnatural—almost—God forgive me—divine. And the thought that this beautiful girl wanted me to kiss her carried me away. Every part of me tensed then relaxed as her hair brushed my cheek. The sound of her breathing and smell of her sweet warm breath made me dizzy. I had dreamed this a million times but never imagined the pleasure a kiss could bring. Not just the kiss but the embrace, every gentle movement of this beautiful girl, holding her in my arms and being held. I kissed her neck and smelled her fragrance, soft and fresh like fine French milled soap. She pressed still closer and when her tongue played with my lips and I opened my mouth slightly, I felt an unbelievable strength and pleasure inside. Kathy's tongue teased and touched, and I embraced her so violently I thought she might break. I reciprocated and she responded pressing her body against me. My shy embarrassment at her knowing my excitement vanished as she breathed warmly in my ear. No more defenses, no more shy inconsequential, inconspicuous, Tweedle Dum. I was Samson and Ulysses and Paris.

There was no longer time for the two of us in that blue Plymouth that night. It simply passed in the fog of intense passion. The pleasure was pure and sinless, and I thought I must be in love and that she must love me to give me so much. We would have many more nights of innocent passion, but in my whole life there could never be such a night again. My life changed that night. I would never again be inconspicuous. I would succeed ,and I would love, and though I thought I would never kiss or love anyone else—

never want to—there would be many other girls with whom I would share the passion I learned from Kathy Crowley.

I drove home that night in a daze of love and lust. I couldn't wait to hold her again. I went to bed but couldn't sleep. Once again I tucked my pillow in the crook of my arm and buried my face in its softness. But this time I wasn't pretending. I was remembering.

Thanks to the missing forty pounds and Kathy Crowley, I recovered in my senior year. In fact I did well enough to get into the University of Notre Dame. I made friends and made up for lost time socially. My yearbook profile summarized my new life: "Brian was a happy-go-lucky individual. The college of his choice will find him a friendly person, good student and an asset to parties."

The fat nerd was gone, forever. But his spirit lives on. There's still an insecure fat little nerd wandering around inside.

Chapter 28.
Notre Dame

Notre Dame! Me at Notre Dame! How many times had I fantasized about coming here? The Golden Dome with Our Lady perched on top, looking down from it's pinnacle; legendary football teams; Knute Rockne, George Gipp. This was the Mecca of Catholic higher education. I was in awe!

At first I had to keep pushing down the annoying question and the insecure indictment: "What am I doing here? This must be a mistake. One day they'll find out and kick me out. Or I'll just flunk out. What am I doing here? Maybe they thought I was my brother or just like my brother." And maybe, after all, I was something like him.

But I pushed it all down. I was here! Room 314 Farley Hall. I had a roommate, Charles T. Bush, III, a moon-faced, privileged nice guy from affluent Gross Point Farms, Michigan; a close friend of the Ford Family. We had little in common and never really got to know each other, but we became friends. I had several roommates over the years. I've kept in touch with Charlie now and then. Tom Heleringer, my roommate for two years, passed away a couple of years ago. I regret not having kept in touch with him. I've lost touch with the others to.

So, this was the place to set my life's course! What was I was to study? What career was I to pursue?

That was decided by fate and some pushing from Dad after my first semester. Fate (with some help from me) had me flunk first semester math. I could probably have survived in the straight Liberal Arts program by taking the course over, but I was shaky, and Dad was there to offer his customary advice. "It's best that you follow your brother. Become a Music Education major. You never have been good at math, and if you fail again, you'll have to repeat the whole year—if they let you stay at all." The push from Dad convinced me the only way to survive college was to follow Bruce even though I was not a musician. (I had already failed piano, clarinet and cymbals). But I could learn. And even if I never was good enough to BE a musician I could always teach. It didn't seem to matter that I had no major instrument. In fact, no instrument at all. I could barely read one line of music, but, in a short time, I'd be expected to compose fugues, inventions, chorales and up to 14 lines of orchestration in three different clefs. The logic was that I wouldn't have to take math, and I could sing.

I became a Music Education major. I learned and composed badly (but good enough to survive). And I sang. My vocal teacher, Father Patrick Maloney, had a national reputation as a coach. He tried hard to make my baritone a tenor and apologized twenty years later. "I really knew it was never to be," he confessed. (I still try and sing up there in the rarified "A-B flat" range but I just scare myself with the shrieking and only try when I'm alone in the car.) I joined the Notre Dame Glee Club and hated it. I didn't like the people. I didn't like the music. I didn't like having to belong.

Bruce was, of course, famous as the Drum Major of the Fighting Irish. He was noted for defying gravity leaning far, far back when strutting down the playing field at the head of the band before each game. When it rained and the field became wet and slippery, people took bets on whether he would fall backwards on his ass. He never did.

It'll Be Okay In The Morning

Once again I was living in his shadow. We didn't see much of each other.

I got a job working in the dining hall kitchen at night mopping floors and steam cleaning the grease traps in the stoves and grilles. The grease succumbed to the steam, and most of it was carried off by the drains. The little bit that remained rose up in the air with the steam and settled in my hair and on my clothes. When finished I felt like a French fry. It was a dirty job.

Ah! But the bread!

Several nights each week they baked fresh bread while we worked. Dozens, scores, hundreds of loaves. And I was allowed to take a still steaming hot loaf back to the dorm.

On Wednesday nights after work I took my loaf and visited Bruce and his roommates in Sorin Hall, and we watched *The Untouchables* on their TV. My admission was that hot loaf of bread. The hard, crackly, tasty crust protected the inside, and when we ravaged the loaf, pealing back that crust, the loaf gave up its sweet, soft, steamy inside. The aroma perfumed the room. We grabbed chunks and slathered on jelly or butter commandeered from the dining hall. Devouring that hot loaf of bread and sneaking an occasional bottle of bourbon into the room was about as exciting as it got at Notre Dame in the late 1950s and early 1960s.

Living on the campus was as close to a monastic existence as one could get without the hooded robe, hair shirt and vow of silence. There was no need for a vow of chastity. That loaf had to compensate for a lot: there were no women, lights were turned out at 10:00 pm each weekday night. We were allowed to stay out until midnight three nights per week but had to check in at chapel each morning before

7:30. During Lent there was no live music on the campus and no sanctioned parties of any kind. And the final blow, the embarrassment to the "Class of 1962," our humiliation, was our storied Fighting Irish football team, the pride of Notre Dame. The legacies of Knute Rockne and George Gipp were dragged through the dying echoes as the team had more consecutive losing seasons and more total loses over those four years than in any four-year period in Notre Dame history prior to or since 1962. To this day I can't watch the Irish play. But I love a loaf of hot bread.

Nevertheless, Notre Dame is uniquely beautiful, peaceful in the spiritual aura of the Grotto and Sacred Heart Cathedral. If you visit you will feel God's calming touch and the soft, gentle breath of "Our Lady" blowing across the campus. It is surely a place God favors. It was the right place for me.

And of all the memories of Notre Dame, the ones I cherished most, the ones that make me smile, are memories of Mrs. Helen Mulrey!

Chapter 29.
Mrs. Helen Mulrey

Winters on the campus were especially grim and dreary. The football season with all its fanfare and excitement ended, leaving a vacuum of silence that, at first was a welcome relief but then became foreboding as if we were all holding our breaths waiting for something to happen—waiting for anything to happen. By late November the winds from Canada carried cold and snow across the Lake Michigan dunes and dumped it all on South Bend. By mid-January the ice accumulation on the sidewalks was so thick it was safer walking on the streets. The ice would be there until May.

After Christmas the situation became desperate. Some of us took short weekend trips to Chicago on the old South Shore railroad that lumbered and clanked right into downtown South Bend like the old Toonerville Trolley. But trips to Chicago were expensive and dangerous for both the students and for Chicago.

I was once left behind in a State Street bar by my brother and his friends. I was drunk and wandered down State Street with one foot on the curb and the other in the slush singing the Notre Dame Fight Song. Fortunately I was rescued by some classmates who recognized me and took me back to their room high up in the Pick Congress Hotel. The group was having great fun throwing furniture out of the 13th story window and peeing on some poor guy who passed out. Such was the danger of weekends in Chicago.

The coming of Lent prompted God and the Church to pile on. Unnecessary roughness! The all-male Catholic campus went into three months of hibernation, reflection and penance in preparation for Easter. Entertainment was curtailed, and all live music was suspended—no parties, no dances, no women, and no fun.

So winters found thousands of young Catholic men involuntarily cooped up on a monastic campus with no place to acceptably express their "maleness" except at Father Lang's Gym or with very few, very prissy, St. Mary's young ladies, or getting drunk at Joer's Bar.

But what else would Notre Dame be if not a place of miracles? And God provided: The blessing was Sarah Ann Mulrey, aka "SAM," and her mother, Helen. Sam went to St. Mary's College, Notre Dame's sister school—a finishing school for good Catholic young women. But Sam was a "townie." She lived in dirty, blue-collar downtown South Bend with her mother, Helen.

Helen loved Notre Dame. She adopted scores of us over the years. She had lived in South Bend since 1940. In 1942 she was deserted by her husband and left alone to raise Sam. She became the Clerk of the Court in South Bend, well known and respected, a loyal fan of Notre Dame and a house mother, match maker, social director, and mother confessor for the scores of ND students who loved her.

My brother Bruce got me my first invitation to Mrs. Mulrey's. As the Drum Major Bruce was a legitimate celebrity on campus, more photographed with more TV close ups than most of the football team. He was one of The Mulreys' favorites.

It'll Be Okay In The Morning

The old Victorian house on East LaSalle Street was only a few blocks from the center of town and in a neighborhood that was threatening to go downhill but wouldn't dare as long as she lived there. Tracks striped the middle of LaSalle Street, and the old South Shore Railroad rambled past Mrs. Mulrey's semi-regularly. She lived there with Sam, her elderly sister, Mary, who suffered from Alzheimer's, and her brother, Walter, who had attended Notre Dame in the early 1900s and ran track.

On one inauspicious Saturday we lost to Purdue by a humiliating score of 51 to 21. It was the worst defeat in Notre Dame history to date. We all needed cheering. I was one of the lucky ones. I got some.

I stopped in front of the address I had been given. I saw no one coming or going. It was quiet, and I wondered if I had the right house. I walked up the five steps onto the large wrap-around front porch and rang the bell. I heard music coming from inside. A few moments later the door opened a crack, and the music squeezed through. I recalled the song "Green Door" from the 1950s, Jim Lowe singing, *"There's an old piano and they play it hot behind the green door. Green door what's that secret you're keeping."* The music was followed by the face of a little old lady as the crack slowly widened. She was smiling, spectacles balanced on the tip of her nose, silver gray hair, cherubic and matronly. She looked up at me with her head cocked to hear. "Excuse me, ma'am, my name is Brian Cosacchi and I was..." And before I could finish, "Well, for heaven's sake, Brian, come on in here," she laughed gently.

The door swung open as if a curtain had been raised on a Broadway show; wall to wall people milling about, everyone smiling, laughing, singing to an old piano in the corner. I tried to take it all in. The house was old, well lived in;

very formal but warm and friendly looking. It had beautiful wood paneling and an entrance foyer with a Persian rug on the hard wood floor. Looking to the right through the partially closed solid oak pocket doors was a comfortable living room with over-stuffed furniture stuffed with people and a cozy coal-burning fire place. To my left was an equal-sized den with the old piano and people holding mugs of beer singing or chatting. It was wonderful. "Ollie, show this young Cosacchi the basement." Mrs. Mulrey gently tugged on a big fellow's sleeve. Ollie Flor was a back-up player on the football team and threw the shot put during track and field season. He nodded obediently and led me through the narrow butler's pantry into the crowded kitchen and then down the stairs to the basement. "So, you're Bruce's kid brother."

"Yeah, I'm a sophomore. I live in Zahm Hall. This is my…"

"Yeah, your brother's a great guy."

"Yeah, I know." I mumbled and swallowed. I thought, "This is great, but I guess I'm destined to always be Bruce's kid brother." It hurt, but I was still grateful. "Have to take the good with the bad," I philosophized. A keg of beer held the place of honor in the musty-smelling old stone basement. It was surrounded by loyal sons of Our Lady. No one was drunk, but it was early.

I thanked Ollie, pulled a 16-ounce cup of beer and began to mill around. I was inconspicuous again, but now it was comfortable. I returned upstairs. Bruce was there in the den holding court, playing the piano and leading the song. He acknowledged my arrival with a wave. I was grateful for my brother that day. Most of the contingent were juniors and seniors and knew each other. I sat and watched TV, sang a little, glanced at pretty girls apparently alone and a few others pressing against their football heroes. I was glad I wasn't in Chicago getting peed on.

At about 8:00 pm people started heading for the kitchen. I followed. The table was weighed down with the biggest ham I had ever seen. Mrs. Mulrey was busy setting out the complements. People helped themselves. It was the best meal I had since leaving home a couple of months before.

The evening matured, and no one got drunk. The kitchen became the forum for people to express themselves on any subject, politely arguing their beliefs. In the den and basement people continued laughter and singing. And in the cozy living room couples dissolved into various soft single shapes silhouetted by the quiet blue coal fire. Tonight I was just a spectator, and I thought. "This is what college should be all about."

It was past eleven o'clock, and all rugged Fighting Irishmen living on campus had to be home, in their cells, before midnight. I dutifully caught the last bus from downtown, checked in with the guard and went to my room. My roommate was asleep. I rolled into bed, smiled and slept well.

For the next three years the Mulrey house was always open to me. Helen never asked for or expected anything in return, but I would have done anything for her and did odd jobs and errands driving about in my 1952 Studebaker with its "now and then" brakes. During the next two years her sister and brother died, and I was honored to be a pallbearer at their funerals. I felt like family.

During my senior year I accepted a scholarship to go on to graduate school to get a master's degree in teaching with a major in counseling.

Brian Cosacchi

After graduation I said good-bye to all my friends. I was left alone. I was frightened to be by myself—on my own. When winter came that year, 1962, along with its ghostly specter, depression spread like a fog over the campus. I had a single room and hunkered down with my studies and my weekly diet of bologna—three pounds for a dollar. I became an expert in the number of ways one could cook it and tried endless combinations. Bologna with peanut butter was a one-time experiment.

I got a job at the campus diner, The Huddle, mopping floors at night after closing, and worked with a little fellow who was studying for his doctoral degree in philosophy. We had little in common aside from mopping, but the weight of winter and the waves of loneliness and self doubt nearly drowned me when I was told he had committed suicide—hanging himself from a door knob with a neck tie in his lonely room. "Oh my God, my dear God, a philosophy doctoral candidate! What use can there be to life if someone like him can't make sense of it?" His suicide that year was followed by a second, an underclassman, who took a swan dive 200 feet from the top of the library.

I spent more time at Mrs. Mulrey's that winter. I brought pizza from Nicola's on Friday nights. I was there on Sundays to break the chain of bologna with her roast beef and potatoes. After dinner she sat me in the big stuffed chair in the living room, and we watched Bonanza together before I headed back. Mrs. Mulrey might have saved my life that year. I loved her! She was Notre Dame's first Heroine.

I finished my master's degree in a year and a summer. I was chomping at the bit to get on with my life and my military obligation was waiting.

Chapter 30.
The Military

The 1077 Army Intelligence Group
When I entered college, the country was at peace. The Korean War was over and Vietnam was a four-year-old French embarrassment. Eisenhower was still President, and yet-to-be President Kennedy wouldn't start our nightmare in Vietnam for three more years.

But in my sophomore year at Notre Dame I joined ROTC; partly because I was afraid of the draft, partly because the Army would actually pay me a little in my junior and senior years, and I needed the money, but mostly because my brother Bruce was in ROTC.

College military was uneventful except for being accused of cheating on an exam in my junior year (I wasn't) and spending my junior year summer at Fort Knox, Kentucky. I won an award as a Distinguished Military Student for fitness activities and just being plain "gung ho."

Real military life began the summer after graduation with three months of Infantry training at Fort Benning, Georgia. Although my assigned branch of service was Army Counterintelligence, all counterintelligence officers were required to complete Infantry training.

The months of June, July and August at Ft. Benning are brutal. Some days the heat was so unbearable we felt as though we were being poached inside our olive-drab, long-sleeved, freshly starched shirts. Sweat soaked our regulation undershirts until they were saturated then, with nothing more to absorb the perspiration, it started running down our arms and legs and backs, soaking our underwear and trousers, dripping through our bloused cuffs and into our military boots until we all just sloshed around.

On the worst days a "heat alert" was declared which required the training officers to refrain from intense physical activities. Sometimes they obeyed the order and sometimes they didn't. On one particularly excruciating day our Company Commander didn't obey, and it cost the lives of two of my fellow Second Lieutenants from heat exhaustion.

I've never been through Marine Basic Training, but I would venture to guess that the physical challenges we faced were similar: 15-mile forced marches in broiling heat, night escape and evasion courses, infiltration courses, crawling on our bellies under barbed wire through sand and mud with live machine gun fire snapping several feet above our frightened butts.

I graduated from Ft. Benning and went on to Ft. Holabird, Maryland, for specialized counterintelligence training. The year was 1963. The training was often boring but occasionally fascinating and fun. Our course in surveillance included how to follow someone without being observed.

During our field training exercise we had to "tail" an instructor through the streets and alleys of downtown Baltimore without getting "burned." I began the real time exercise with confidence. So when my "mark" turned a predictable 180 degrees on the sidewalk, I was ready. And when he crossed the street and re-crossed, I was ready. When he turned to look in the window of a department store, I knew he was looking at reflections. I was prepared for all the moves. I followed him into a department store knowing this would be difficult. Would he look for an alternate exit? Would he merge with the crowd and lose himself? I followed him from a distance, keeping a close eye. I pretended to shop, passing by display bins but never looking directly down at the merchandise for fear I might lose him. I moved from one table to the next reaching down pretending to inspect whatever it was on the table but keeping an eye on the instructor. Then, our eyes met only for a moment. He was smiling at me! I was "burned!" How could I be? I had been so careful. I glanced up at people close by. They were smirking or moving away as they watched me fingering a display of women's bras. Ooops! The instructor laughed.

He gave me a good grade nonetheless.

Death of The President
We were in Ms Kleka's typing class on that Friday in late November when the Major broke in and notified us that the President had been shot. We were dumbstruck. How could this happen? Where was our intelligence? Of course it was the Russians in reprisal for the Cuban Blockade. We didn't know. We were just ranting like the rest of the country, but as special Counterintelligence agents, we felt a sick embarrassment. The President died a few hours later.

Being stationed in Baltimore made it easy to get to D.C. and to be among the hundreds of thousands who passed solemnly by the catafalque in the Capitol Rotunda. We three roommate lieutenants, Brian Cosacchi, Pat Giles and Charlie Giersch, flowed slowly with the endless stream of mourners. So many tears, so much deep, heartfelt sadness for someone they didn't know. Muffled sobs echoed from the rotunda's dome—grief that would normally be reserved for close relatives shed for this man who had led us for such a short while. We became part of this massive mourning and decided to return and attend the funeral the following day, November 25, 1963.

It was particularly cold on the morning of the funeral, but the sun was bright. We dressed in our "greens" and decided to wear our white dress gloves because of the formality of the occasion. We left early, anticipating a huge crowd and the difficulty finding parking.

We found a place to park and began the trek toward the church. Crowds had already gathered behind the police line of wooden barricades along the funeral procession's route. The only people walking behind the barricades were police and military—AND MILITARY! We looked at each other, put on our official looking white gloves, stepped around the barricade and began to walk toward the church. We didn't consider the possible consequences of crashing the police line. We were just three innocent second lieutenants going to attend the President's funeral. As we walked, we saluted a flow of senior officers; 'bird' colonels and lots of generals! I got a little squeamish. Surely we'd be stopped, questioned, perhaps arrested, thrown into jail, interrogated, maybe implicated in the murder of the President and spend the rest of our lives in prison or maybe even executed, hanged by the neck. Too late to turn back now. But it was getting easier. Just look 'em in the eye and salute.

The crowds to our left lined up along the street behind the barricades 10 to15 deep. Except for the stream of generals, we were the only ones on the sidewalk, and before we knew it, we were standing in front of Saint Matthew's Cathedral.

The three of us separated, not wanting to draw attention. There were dozens of square-jawed "Dick Tracys" with little tell-tale Secret Service lapel pins swarming all around

It'll Be Okay In The Morning

the church entrance. Two of them stood right next to me whispering into their cuffs and palms of their hands, scanning the roof tops and the growing crowd. I braced a stiff, formal parade rest trying to look official. I set my jaw and peeked out from under the visor of my hat. People gathered behind me, high-ranking officers and dignitaries. They must have presumed I was a guard, and I accepted the role. I was beginning to enjoy myself and my little game. The funeral cortege was not expected for twenty minutes.

I shifted from attention to Parade Rest now and then to prevent cramping. On one of these changes I glanced down at the sidewalk. Something was written in chalk. I was looking at it upside down. I flipped it in my head. Scoop? Shoot? No, Shoup. SHOUP, the Marine Corps Commandant and member of the Joint Chiefs of Staff. There, to my left, a little closer to the church, the name Taylor. General Maxwell Taylor, Chairman of the Joint Chiefs. I was standing where General Shoup and the Joint Chiefs were supposed to stand any minute.

I pushed back against the "Dick Tracy" behind me. He eased backwards admonishing those behind him, "Step back, please." Just a few minutes later the Generals appeared out of nowhere. They just walked out of the crowd ,and in a moment I was standing just behind him, General David Shoup, Commandant of the Marine Corps and close enough to General Taylor for him to smell my frightened breath. And no one said a word.

The entourage arrived. I watched as the casket was carried into the church, followed by the family and the long line of foreign heads of state and other notables. The funeral Mass was shared with the crowd standing outside in the cold via a PA system. Not another sound was heard. Thousands of people gathered standing shoulder to shoulder and yet not a sound, as if God had pushed the mute button. We all could hear Cardinal Cushing and the mournful but uplifting music. I was glad I came, glad I was standing where I was.

The funeral ended. The mourners exited the church, and the black limousines arrived to pick up their appointed dignitaries, like links of a chain. I was close enough to reach out and touch them as they passed. As each link of the chain stopped, a military attendant opened the rear door and saluted as the dignitary entered; then he closed the door after him. One after another they left in organized timely succession. But then a slight bottleneck. The limousine for King Baudouin of Belgium waited for an attendant to open the door. I thought, *They need someone to open that limo door! Why not me?* I stepped forward and just did it, white gloves and all. I escorted King Baudouin into his limousine at JFK's funeral. And no one said a word.

Boston Military

When we entered Ft. Holabird for Intelligence training, we also received our post training assignments. Most of us worried about being sent to Vietnam even though the war was still in its infancy. The assignments were posted one morning. I approached the bulletin board. *May I have the envelope please* crossed my mind as I looked at the list, Clark, Corwin, Cosacchi—my eyes followed the line across. I squinted to ease the blow. 1077 INTC Group—Boston, MA.

Boston! God was looking good today.

The world was in turmoil, and I got to go to Boston for the remainder of my military career. I actually felt guilty. My roommate Pat Giles joined me. We graduated Ft. Holabird in January and made straight for Boston—for the good times.

It'll Be Okay In The Morning

We found a funky apartment on the far side of Beacon Hill on Pinckney Street just up the hill from Louisburg Square where the Kennedy's kept a town house. Very swank! Our first night in the apartment we had a little party with three girls and no furniture. It was a bachelor's paradise—and I was engaged. Ah, the pity of it all.

We worked out of the Boston Army Base, an old, dumpy, brick warehouse-looking building not far from Old South Station. The work was routine for the most part, conducting background investigations on people requiring top-secret clearance. But the monotony was broken by one extraordinary assignment for all 30 of us in the Boston 1077th INTC.

The Army's Counterintelligence Corps (CIC), was the Army's defense against foreign espionage and domestic sedition. But we also trained our own espionage agents to go behind the Iron Curtain to gather information. Once each year our INTC Group conducted a training exercise for these people—a practical exercise—a final exam. Boston became a crossing point into "East Germany." The training exercise objective for the students was to cross into "East Germany" (AKA Boston) without detection, contact their sources using a different identity, obtain certain information from them and return to "West Germany" (AKA Ft. Holabird).

Our job was to harass them, catch them and subject them to intense interrogation. But the game was rigged to make it impossible for them to finish without being caught. We knew who they were. We had photos of them and knew where they were staying. If they weren't prepared when they stepped down off the train at South Station, they were immediately arrested.

My partner in the training exercise was Henry Shephardson (Shep) Wild, III, a distinguished Yale graduate whose family founded The Scovill Manufacturing Company in Waterbury, Connecticut. Affable and engaging with a bit of a blue-blood air, Shep was fun to work with.

At 7:55 Monday morning, the train from "West Germany" arrived on time. Our first victim was on that train. He wasn't prepared. We spotted him before his feet hit the pavement. We walked in his direction. He gave us an "Oh s—t" look and began to glance around, looking for an exit or a hole to swallow him. No use. We confronted him and showed him our credentials: East German Police. We asked him for his identification, but it really didn't make any difference. We arrested him and hauled him off to Sergeant Tardiff, our interrogator. Tardiff licked his lips and cackled. He loved his work.

We went looking for number two.

We missed #2 at the station. No problem. We asked the training cadre where he was staying and headed to The Parker House Hotel on School Street.

The Parker House was built in 1855 and is still the Grand Dame of Boston Hotels. It gave its name to those wonderful little rolls that accompany special holiday meals. Uniformed bell hops scurried around the enormous baroque lobby with baggage and messages for guests. Thick carpets, comfortable furniture, heavy, dark carved wooden moldings and furnishings gave the place it's moneyed, cultured look. My partner had that same moneyed, cultured look. He fit in well when he asked in what room our #2 was staying. The desk clerk didn't bat an eye. "That would be, ahem—Room 642, sir."

It'll Be Okay In The Morning

We took the elevator to the sixth floor. The hallways in this grand old hotel were wider than Boston City streets, with high ceilings, carpets like fresh snow absorbing soft whispers, walls with formal sconces holding dim lights in keeping with the snobby quiet.

We cruised down the hallway noting the room numbers as we passed and eyeing the Parker House clientele as they eyed us; evening gowns, tuxedos, lavaliere jewelry and pince nez.

Room 642. The old hotel had been built long before air conditioning. Almost a century later the rooms hadn't been remodeled. They came with transom windows above the doors that opened and closed from the inside for ventilation. We saw the light was on. # 2 was in there! I knocked. No response. I knocked again and again, no response. This time I knocked harder, louder and stated our business, "Open up, East German Police." Passers by gave us startled looks. Finally a response, "ohm, ah, (yawn), just a minute you woke me—just a minute."

We knew something was going on in there. Shep faced the door, leaned against it and offered his knee. I scrambled up and peeked over the open transom into the lighted room. Passers-by gawked in shocked disapproval and went harumphing on down the hallway.

#2 was sitting at the tiny desk they squeezed into the expensive, tiny room. He was making yawning noises as he frantically shuffled things on the desk. "(Yawn), ohhhhh, ha, ho, coming," He jumped up from the desk with something in his hands, scrambled to the old fashioned radiator and stuffed the items somewhere behind. I jumped down from my perch just before he slid the chain lock back and disengaged the dead bolt. The door opened. He feigned drowsiness, "Wah, wasamatter, whadyawant, who are you anyway?" We showed him our credentials. I moved past him and surveyed the room. He looked relieved, safe, at ease. The look turned to shock when I moved straight to the radiator, reached behind, found the hole he had cut in the wall, and pulled out his phony passport and a Minox camera. We arrested him and fed him to Sergeant Tardiff.

Two down—one to go!

Two days, twenty cups of coffee, six hours of sleep, and no sign of #3. It made us irritable and smelly. We checked with the desk clerk in the cheap hotel. He told us, yes, he had indeed slept in his room the past two nights. Housekeeping had made up his room each morning. We were frustrated and angry and made a stupid decision. We called our Operations Officer and asked him to send our DAME guy (Defense Against Methods of Entry). Technically the DAME guy protects our people from having bugs placed in their rooms, but their real job was to break into rooms of foreign dignitaries and place listening devices.

He arrived with a smile. The three of us clustered in private and discussed the situation. He gently warned us that what we wanted to do was against the rules of the exercise, but he would defer to our orders since he was only a warrant officer. The three of us pretended to leave. Instead we found the staircase and trotted up to #3's room.

The hallways were quiet. We were nervous and excited. Our DAME guy removed the little leather tool kit from his sport coat's vest pocket, glanced around for a moment and began to work. It only took a few seconds. We were in. We would find incriminating evidence, then wait for #3 and arrest him. We began a methodical search. But as we were rifling through his luggage, the door opened. It was the hotel manager—a short, balding, overweight, sloppy-looking man with a ridiculous comb over wearing a motley sport coat, just big enough to fit around his waist, but the sleeves almost reached his knuckles.

"What the hell do you think you're doing? Who the hell are you?" He may have been fat and sloppy, but he took his job seriously. I considered telling him "We're East German Secret Police and we are tracking an American spy." But he probably wouldn't see the humor, and I didn't want our East German Police training story to wind up on the front page of the Boston Globe. Shep and I kept our mouths shut and let the DAME guy do the talking. He had lots of practice. But the manager wasn't buying and insisted on talking to our commanding officer, Major Chalowpowski. He called headquarters and had a muttered conversation with the Major. Then he handed the phone to the manager. As the manager listened, we watched his demeanor change from a turbulent tornado to a calm breeze. In thirty seconds his expression changed from anger to conciliation, to humor, to abject apology. I thought he was going to salute before he hung up. The Major averted a public relations debacle and saved the skins of two idiot second lieutenants playing cops and robbers.

When we returned to our Headquarters at the Boston Army Base, we presented ourselves to the Major and received a well deserved but controlled chewing-out. Our evaluations for the six-month period reflected the Major's disappointment.

I only had nine months left to serve. I was engaged to be married; new responsibilities. I knew I'd better clean up my act.

Chapter 31.
Getting Married

Two Lost Souls

The notion that two people serendipitously trip over each other and discover they were meant to spend eternity together to the exclusion of all others is romantic fantasy.

I think most people first fall in lust. Then, depending on their age, biological clock and need for some kind of companionship, they take the plunge. There isn't a lot of attention paid to long-term compatibility. So two people with completely different backgrounds, life experiences, personalities and goals can make a lifetime commitment to each other and figure out what love is along the way.

Les and I have been trying to figure out the love thing along the way for 46 years.

I found Les after Kathy and Beth and Dottie and Karen and Honey and Carol. My friend Pat DeSena had been dating Les but wanted to break off and asked me to help by asking Les out. I thought he was nuts—couldn't see a good thing. I was happy to oblige. I asked her out. She said yes. It was winter, and it began to snow the night of our first date. I didn't want to miss this chance to see her, so I went to pick her up in spite of the snow. By the time I reached her home, the roads were too hazardous to chance driving anywhere unless an emergency. Les and her parents suggested we just hang out at their home. We did. We were left alone. We watched TV and chatted and—and—I kissed her—and she didn't mind. It didn't take many more dates for physical chemistry to sweep us away. But we had very little in common.

Les' parents were sophisticated, intellectual, artistic, successful, attractive with WASPy names and backgrounds: Putney and Urban. And, at least from outward appearances, they were well to do. They were comfortable with their cocktails and fashion and dinner parties.

My parents were Old World, alcoholic, volatile, earthy, and they were comfortable in their bathrobes and underwear. But they made sure their children understood there was another world of sophistication and cocktails, even if they didn't belong in it. I learned to pretend to be part of it.

So as long as I kept my parents in the closet, I could range out among the beautiful people and awkwardly fit in. Notre Dame helped hone the fraud.

Les and I fell in lust. We needed each other, or at least we needed someone. If it wasn't love, I thought that would come in time and I really had no idea what love was.

I rarely let my parents out of the closet, afraid of being found out. I'm ashamed to say I was embarrassed by them: the alcoholic shanty Irish colleen and little Calabrese penguin.

But sooner or later Les had to visit our home to meet Mom. On this day Mom was sitting in her favorite well-worn easy chair—the one with the doilies hiding most of the thread-bare holes. Her sewing basket was cradled between her legs, her housecoat stretched between her knees. She was trying to pin some plastic flowers on an old hat. Her tongue jutted from the corner of her mouth reflecting the intense effort and the fact that she must have had a snort or two before we arrived. To me she was Aunt Minnie Pearl. I cringed. I thought, *Les will never marry the son of Aunt Minnie Pearl. Her parents would never let her.*

But to Les, Mom was Martha Stewart, creative, artistic in a crafty way. She couldn't see the truth about Mom. She told me when we left, "I didn't realize your mother was so into crafts and millinery." I smiled and nodded.

We were married in Harrison in the church of St. Gregory the Great. Les' parents were agnostic or atheist. They didn't go to church, but they felt taking photos in a church was wrong, so we had no pictures of our wedding. Since neither of us had any close friends, only immediate family attended: all my Italian aunts and uncles and a couple of Les' distant relatives.

Instead of a reception Les and I, along with just our parents, had dinner at Tappan Hill, an extraordinarily beautiful restaurant overlooking the Hudson River. I wasn't very hungry and kept waiting for something to go wrong. Tommy Manville, a roguish elderly multimillionaire celebrity, was sitting at a nearby table with his sixth or seventh wife. He sent the Maitre d' over to extend his compliments to the groom on his selection of such a beautiful wife. I was glad he noticed. Yes she was. Nothing went wrong, and we began our tumultuous life together.

Forty-six years of getting to know each other. Forty-six years of frequently asking ourselves, "Why did I do this again?" The differences we played down or refused to acknowledge in the beginning have constantly precipitated vocal disagreements during our journey—a barrier to real simpatico. I'm a Cosacchi, comfortable in my underwear. Les is an Urban and needs to look and do and be right and wants everything around her to be—just so.

And the same differences have contributed to a rich variety of ideas and created two individuals with a greater appreciation of differences and compromise and the value of life itself. The differences could have destroyed us, and maybe they will one day, but we've found a way to make it work for us. God knows we've muddled and muscled through a panoply of potential pitfalls.

Newlyweds
Our honeymoon was not a great beginning. Les experienced a severely strained neck riding around Bermuda on a Moped. This made our repeated marital consummations awkward. Then, when we returned to the airport, we discovered that all the money given to us by my relatives had been stolen from the glove compartment of our car. But we put it aside. There would be better days ahead. We moved into our apartment in West Haven, Connecticut.

I had been appointed officer in charge of the Connecticut office of Army Counterintelligence. Nobody else in Boston wanted the job. I really didn't know what I was doing. And while I was responsible for supervising nine special agents and my secretary, they all really supervised me. The job consisted mostly of conducting background investigations on individuals needing Army security clearances.

Thank God we weren't worried about terrorists at that time. Those were relatively innocent days, and the worst of what we dealt with were a few mal-content anti-Vietnam activists matriculating to Yale.

The job was easy.

It was my new marriage that presented the challenges and has continued to for more than 45 years.

The first collision of our differences left me with a pathetic, confounded *Huh?* expression, like a big, dumb bulldog cartoon character being whacked on the side of the head with a frying pan or having a stick of dynamite go off in his hand. *Huh?* Kaboom! The adversary was always

It'll Be Okay In The Morning

some little teeny mouse or a Tweety Bird. Crash! *Huh?!* with a "questilimation mark."

Before we were married we agreed that while we had many differences, we loved each other, and we would have lots of time to argue after we were married. It was prophetic! Have we ever! And we joked about it at the time.

I believed that after we were married, my role would be that of unquestioned leader and head of the household. I assumed that role would be accepted and respected. I thought it my duty to call the shots.

Then one particularly stormy night about a month after returning from our honeymoon we had a disagreement. The issue has long since been forgotten. But it was a direct challenge to my role as King, and there was some principle or other to uphold.

I insisted on imposing my decision. But Les, in very few words and without using any improper language whatever, said clearly, "Fuck you and your castle. I'm doing it my way." And it began:

"No you're not!"
"Yes I am!"
"No you're not!"
"Yes I am!"
"No you're not!"
"Yes I am!"
"No you're not!"
"Yes I am!"

She fled to the bedroom. I followed. We yelled, and she stormed out of the room, leaving me yelling at the cat with a *Huh?* look on my confounded face.

A moment later I heard the apartment door slam. I thought, *But it's pouring outside. She couldn't have gone outside.*

Then, without conviction, *Well, that'll teach her.* Then, with a hint of conciliation, *Maybe I was a little harsh. Maybe I should have tried to see her side. But it's my job! I'm supposed to be the Head here! I wonder where she went? I hope she's all right. Wasn't that stupid of her to run out in this downpour? Serves her right! She'll be back in a minute. It's pouring out there.*

One minute, three, five, ten. The soliloquy ended with, *Where the heck is she?* with such a perfect blend of anger and fear that I wasn't sure what I felt.

Damn, I better go find her. I ran out the door into a deluge and a pitch-black night. There was no more anger, just fear. I yelled her name over the clamor, now desperate, thinking she could be dead or worse, she might leave me.

But she wasn't dead, just resolutely waiting, drenched under the broad umbrella of a tulip tree. It was clear, there would be no King in our home, only a Queen with a lackey. She made the point by having me beg her to return to the apartment. "But you'll freeze or drown out here. You have to come back inside. I insist!" No response. "Please, pleeeeaaaaase come back. I—I—I'm sorry." She finally demurred, and I led her back. There was no conversation—no King—only a benevolent Queen.

Sure, now and then she has to take out the frying pan. Whack! Boing! *Huh?!* And so it's been.

Chapter 32.
Leaving the Military Womb—On Our Own

After the trauma of realizing who we married and accepting it, we settled comfortably into life in New Haven—Les working at the Winchester Division of Olin Mathieson and me as officer in charge of the Connecticut office of Army Counterintelligence.

The months dragged by, but with the spring of 1965 blossomed the realization that I would be out of a job in a few months. No more educational or military wombs to hide in. I had two degrees in Education. But I knew that as a teacher, even if I were a good one, which I wasn't, I could never give Les what she and her parents expected for her. Old insecurity filled me up again. What could I possibly do to be successful?

I convinced myself I wanted a job in business, even though I knew nothing about it. Me, a first generation, Irish/Italian music major with a master's degree in counseling! I'd be out of place—out of my league, and everyone around me would know it. I'd see it in the way they looked at me—talked behind my back—snickered. Aside from shoveling snow and selling lemonade when I was ten, I didn't know anything about business. I was sure it required very special skills—very brainy people with a lot of complicated secrets like the laws of physics and special skills like brain surgeons. I didn't know any of this, and I couldn't ask, or I'd be exposed as a fraud. So I would have to fake it—pretend to be smart.

If I could pull it off, it seemed to be a better way to make a living. Les would be proud, and maybe her father would give me credit for half a brain.

I wanted a job in personnel. I thought I could still help people. I could use my counseling skills. I wrote and rewrote my resume, embellishing on my life but keeping it mostly honest. We mailed dozens and sealed each with an optimistic prayer. I looked forward to the mail and jumped each time the phone rang. Finally, *the* letter, my big chance: an interview for a job in personnel with General Foods. It had one catch—the position was at their Gaines Pet Food plant and corn mill in Kankakee, Illinois—a place not noted for its culture and nightlife. But it would be a beginning. After all, how much worse could it be than South Bend in the winter?

After a day of interviews they made me an offer. I grabbed it. Once again, I got another job nobody else wanted.

And at the end of June 1965 I received my honorable discharge from the service. I didn't really want to leave. I liked my job: great independence, lots of responsibility, and we were well taken care of. But a Vietnam assignment was a strong possibility, so I chose the business jungle. Vietnam might have been easier. This business jungle was innocent looking, but it was dark and dangerous behind all the smiles and hand shakes.

I didn't have the right weapons, no map. No one told me where the minefields were or what the enemy looked like. I could never tell who my allies were. There were always several battles going on at once with lots of different interests fighting for more.

I was frightened.

It'll Be Okay In The Morning

I had a wife and would someday have children, and if I couldn't hack it—if I didn't succeed—I worried we would all be found one day, starving, face down in the gutter, choking to death in our own puke. I could see it. I knew it could really happen if I failed.

June 28, 1965. I reported to General Foods Corporate Headquarters for my one-month indoctrination before heading to gulag Kankakee with Les.

In 1965 General Foods was the 25th largest company in the United States. Its headquarters reflected its muscle: an enormous, austere rambling three-story brick building in White Plains, New York.

I parked my little 1964 Rambler in the visitor's parking lot and stopped for a moment to consider what was ahead. I took a deep breath. "David and Goliath" crossed my mind. The entry waited, and I entered the dragon's mouth. No turning back now.

Polished granite floors, impressive open lobby with a giant 8-foot-high brass "GF" in the center and all around in little show cases the well known host of General Foods products: Maxwell House and Sanka coffee, Jell-O, Post Cereals, Birds Eye, Gaines, Minute Rice and a variety of lesser brands.

I tried to feel confident in my recently purchased dark blue suit. But the harder I tried, the worse I felt. *Have I got the right shirt on? Do I look too Italian—too Irish—too short—too fat? Oh my God, is my fly open?* I approached the impeccably dressed and coiffed receptionist. I smiled, and she cheerfully, dutifully, pleasantly, confidently smiled back. I didn't feel confident. I was sure my fly was open. I was sure there was a giant goober perched on the edge of my nostril and some spinach stuck to my upper incisors. I was sure I would spit on her if I tried to say anything, and a little spittle splashed on her when I came to the "Cosacchi" part of "my name is." She never batted an eye. She smiled, "Mr. Crable is expecting you. Please have a seat. Miss Maddox will be right down." I responded like an idiot, saying something lunatic like, "Thank you so extremely much for your most utmost cordiality and receptionisting," then cursed myself and wished I could do it over again and that I could disappear. I retreated and sank into an uncomfortable, cold vinyl chair. Beads of sweat blossomed on my brow. My underarms became a swamp, wetting my shirt to my waist. "I don't belong here. I know it. They know it. I'm an idiot, and my fly must be open."

"Mr. Cosacchi?" I looked up and felt better. "I'm Mary Jane Maddox, Mr. Crable's Secretary. He's expecting you. Won't you come this way please?"

She was lovely—professional—but very pleasant with a smile that would end winter. She had just the right amount of make-up; just the right shoulder-length hair draped forward framing her lovely, well organized features. Her attire was business reserved. But she needed nothing more.

"How was the trip from—New Haven, is it?"

"Yes, fine, uneventful, thanks." We chatted politely as we walked. The building was a labyrinth of crisscrossing hallways, staircases, and hundreds of cloned single-windowed offices.

"How long have you been with GF?...Have you far to commute?"

It'll Be Okay In The Morning

She reciprocated, "What did you do in the Service?... Does Mrs. Cosacchi work also?"

We stopped in front of an office in the unending line. The nameplate read, "A.L. Crable." Mary Jane stepped inside. "Mr. Cosacchi is here, Mr. Crable." No response. I felt a chill. I could see inside, and he could see out.

Sitting behind a cluttered desk was a slightly portly man in his late forties. He had rugged features, deep creases in his jowly, humorless face. He was nearly bald with a pathetic comb-over that began somewhere around his left ear. His well-worn brown suit was wrinkled, his tie askew. I thought, *I don't think he's happy I'm here.*

He motioned me in and Mary Jane out with the same sweep of his hand. The smoke from the cigarette between his fingers rose up to attack my eyes and nose. He squinted, choked and coughed a bit as he continued to motion. "Well, come on in then." I was alone, and the angel Mary was gone.

I sat. He returned to the work at hand on his desk leaving an awkward, impolite silence. Finally he looked up. "So, Brian, you're going off to Kankakee." He paused, looked at me and concealed an obvious smile, cupping his hand over his mouth. "Well, we'll do our best to get you ready." With that he handed me a piece of paper that detailed a day-by-day schedule for my month's orientation.

"Check in with me every morning. I'm usually here by 7:30. Any problems, let Mary Jane know. Any questions—things that aren't clear—come and see me at the end of the day. I usually don't leave until 6:15." He went on to show me an organization chart of the corporation. I got lost somewhere on the third level of the line-and-box chart but didn't want to say. So I just kept nodding. I had to try and at least look smart.

The month passed quickly. I had questions but never went to Mr. Crable. I gained a little confidence. Maybe I wasn't totally stupid. Maybe I could learn.

Les and I said our goodbyes to our families and left on our first great adventure. We couldn't know how often and how hard our love would be tested in all the years to come.

Chapter 33.
Kankakee, Illinois

No one really knows what the name *Kankakee* means. Some think it means "wonderful land." I don't know where those people would have come from. Some think it means "swamp," perhaps more apropos!

In the middle of the 19th century the city of Kankakee had to make a decision that would determine its future, its character, its economy and its culture. The people had to choose: Kankakee could become either the home of the University of Illinois or the home of the Illinois Mental Hospital. The Mental Hospital offered more job opportunities. So in 1966 there was no theatre in Kankakee, no museums, no symphony, no first class medical facility, no respected seat of learning. There was just corn and crazy people.

We drove the roughly 1,000 miles in our treasured 1964 American Motors Rambler. The trip was forgettable. We were thinking about our new home, the job, the career, our future together.

We drove into town from the north on the two-lane highway that stretched on straight ahead forever. The highest thing on the horizon in any direction was the railroad trestle rising perhaps 6 or 7 feet above the road keeping us company for the last 100 miles.

Conversation was lacking, but we were both thinking the same thing. *This looks flat and boring.* I hoped the people were not like the landscape. I felt a little snobbish—a little regretful. I couldn't let Les see.

We checked into the pretentiously named Imperial Motel, the best Kankakee had to offer with vibrating bed, purple shag carpets, real imitation wood paneling and plastic water glasses. The manager greeted us warmly. "If there's anything you need—anything at all, please call me. We really appreciate General Foods and all it does for Kankakee." I realized how important GF was to the community. I realized how much more important it would be when the Gainesburger Plant started up in five months—how important my job was, hiring more than 500 more people in this little town. GF was a big fish in a little pond. My job would be important. I was encouraged. And as for Kankakee, well it wouldn't be forever.

We settled in and took hold a little more each day. Kankakee was close to nowhere and seemed as far from the beautiful ocean and sandy beaches of Long Island Sound as we could get and still be in this country. No green hills, no green forests, no skiing, no swimming, just corn and crazy people.

But we would make the best of it. A couple of years here wouldn't be so bad—a good investment in our future. There was no turning back; no yellow brick road, no wizard, just scarecrows here and there guarding the endless stretches of cornfields.

We looked for something familiar to bring us closer to home, something comforting. One of our first ideas was food! Italian food!

An Italian restaurant would remind us of home. Maybe we couldn't expect Kankakee to equal the food of Leon's,

It'll Be Okay In The Morning

our favorite New Haven ristorante, or the pizza at Pepe's or Sally's where people had to stand in line for hours. But even a mediocre checkered table cloth, Guinea/Wop, Mom-and-Pop joint with empty Chianti bottles wrapped in straw hanging from the walls would be comforting and reassuring—a touch of home.

Some local residents recommended a place called Mantone's. They said it was the best I-talian food for miles. The *I-talian* pronunciation of Italian raised my antennae as I had always ascribed that "I" emphasis to people whose taste in Italian food was limited to Chef Boyardee. But I wanted to believe Italian food would be one small common denominator.

We drove the 10 miles of two-lane highway South from Kankakee. There was little to see, just miles of corn and soy and modest farmhouses set discreetly far back from the road. Mantone's was easy to find. A single story blah-looking building; cinder block and Texture 111 painted dirt brown. A large red neon sign with *Mantone's* written in script was a classy greeting. The building sat forlorn-looking in an enormous dirt-and-gravel parking lot with enough room for a hundred cars. On this evening there were only four or five, and I reasoned, *It's early and it's Tuesday. But if this is the quality of the outside, what's the inside like—what will the food be like?* I brushed the concern away like flicking bird poop off my shoulder. It left a little stain. I forced myself to think, "Come on, the best Italian restaurants are unpretentious, homey, folksy. It'll be great."

The inside was true to its exterior: cheap wood paneling, a plastic imitation crystal chandelier hanging from the center of an already low ceiling. Two very inexpensive prints caught my eye: the first, a view of the Isle of Capri painted in iridescent colors so that it almost jumped off the wall. "The

Isle of Capri" was printed below in four-inch high letters. The other print was an equally colorful painting of Vesuvius or Stromboli erupting and spewing smoke and lava into the air.

Only three tables were occupied.

A smiling, middle-aged man whom I guessed was the owner approached, "How many will there be?" he asked as if there was some huge entourage trailing in behind us.

"Just the two of us," I smiled back. We were escorted to a table against a wall far from the other diners. We ordered drinks and were handed paper menus. As I opened mine, I noticed it was speckled, stained with marinara sauce. I forgivingly thought, *How typically "Mom and Pop," really down to earth, this is what real down home Italian should be.*

I opened the menu. The bottom fell out! No more happy thoughts. I looked at Les. She had already opened her menu. She looked back with an *eh?* expression.

The list of entrées was brief, beginning with "Spaghetti and Tomato Sauce." I thought, *Tomato Sauce! Who eats spaghetti with tomato sauce? Marinara or maybe Bolognese, or something, but tomato sauce comes out of a can! This must be some local thing—a Midwestern term.*

I read on:
Spaghetti and Tomato Sauce
Spaghetti and Meatballs
Spaghetti and Sausage
Lasagna with Tomato Sauce

It'll Be Okay In The Morning

That was about the extent of the Italian entrees. There were a few purely American dishes: steak and some kind of fish or other.

But I wanted Italian. In fact I wanted my favorite Italian dish available on virtually every Italian restaurant menu. I wanted veal Parmesan! I motioned to the waiter/owner. "Are you ready to order sir?"

"Ahh," I began, "We just moved here from back East, and we used to go to Italian restaurants a lot. I couldn't help notice that your menu doesn't include veal Parmesan. Is it something you prepare on request?"

"We'd be happy to prepare your favorite dish for you, Sir. How shall I tell the chef to prepare it?"

Oh no, he doesn't know what it is, I thought. And before I could check myself, I blurted, "Well, you know, ahh, veal Parmesan, it's a fillet of veal pounded thin with mozzarella and marinara—ahh—tomato sauce on top."

"Ah, of course, and for you, Ma'am?" Les played it safe and ordered a steak. We sipped our drinks and waited. Our salads came served in plastic, imitation-wood bowls. If the salty, tasteless dressing didn't come out of a bottle, it should have. I picked at the greens half expecting to find something crawling down there below the cheap head lettuce. We made small talk, joked about the menu, the restaurant, Kankakee, the dog food plant.

The door to the kitchen pushed open, and here came the owner/waiter, tray on shoulder. I didn't want to look, but I did. Les' strip streak looked very nice as he placed it before her. He made his way to my side of the table and lowered the dish to the table in front of me. I was so embarrassed for

Mantone's Restaurant at what sat in front of me I couldn't say anything except. "Thank you."

I looked down at my veal Parmesan; a deep fried, tenderized, heavily breaded veal patty—the kind you get in greasy, gravy-covered, cheap Banquet dinners or on school lunch menus. It sat on the plate and stared at me through a splash of watery tomato sauce that looked and smelled like tomato juice. The whole thing was topped with a nice thick slice of cold Mozzarella.

I almost laughed as I thought, *I wonder what they would have served if I ordered Chicken Parmesan.*

I ate a little to be polite and paid the bill, which would have been very reasonable if the food had been edible.

I'd make my own Italian food from now on.

Chapter 34.
Adjusting to Dog (Food) Days

After the shock of Mantone's, we learned. We got the message. This was Kankakee, Illinois, the middle of the middle of Middle America. All the menus here were limited: food, culture, education, exercise, employment, housing, religion, even sex. Not that we were in any position to be choosey on our combined salaries of $12,000, but it would have been nice if La Choy wasn't the only Chinese alternative to Chun King; if people didn't think Julius LaRosa was history's most famous Italian or that people from just up the road in Peatone weren't "foreigners."

We searched around, talked to other dazed transplants and once we understood "drab can be beautiful," we became more comfortable. Actually, resigned might better apply.

Life became routine. Les worked as a secretary, and I was the employment specialist for the new Gaines Dog Food Plant and Corn Mill. The job consisted of supplying warm bodies to the production manager whenever he called. General Foods had gambled big-time on the success of new technology called soft-moist processing—Gaines Burgers to you. The plant had to expand from 700 to 1200 souls between October 1965 and January 1966: 500 new people in four months.

Kankakee was an industrial town of about 30,000, and business was booming for everyone. The town was enjoying near full employment. Finding people willing to slop around in stomach-churning raw material that became dog food wasn't easy. The Gaines ads said, "Made from 100% meat." And so it was: chopped up horse guts all yellow, green and iridescent purple. Open gondola cars arrived at our rail siding with thousands and thousands of disembodied chicken heads and feet—millions of accusing dead chicken eyes staring up from their mass grave.

Nevertheless, General Foods offered the best pay and benefits in town, and the company name garnered respect from the community, so the applications came pouring in. On Monday morning, after running a weekend ad, the waiting room was shoulder-to-shoulder applicants.

For the first month I tried to do due diligence to the employment process. No one could take an application home as that invariably meant someone else filled it out. All applicants who were called in, which meant anyone who could spell their name and had a phone, had to take an intelligence test—the Wonderlic Test: A test to determine the learning and problem-solving skills of the applicant. We had an arbitrary passing grade and began interviewing and hiring approximately one in six who took the test.

So, on Thursday afternoon when the production manager asked for 40 people for Monday morning, I had to screen 240 people over the next three days. Needless to say the standards quickly came down—and down—and down. Eventually we stopped giving the test, but we never ran out of people, and the plant started up successfully.

Life was a continuing challenge.

It'll Be Okay In The Morning

Each business quarter the plant manager convened a management meeting for the nearly 200 management employees. The objective was to review the prior quarter's results and the coming quarter's objectives. But in that new age of "sensitivity training," functional integration and business enlightenment, it was also to improve rapport between operations and administration. The rotten job of coordinator for these events was mine: selecting the site, the menu, negotiating the open bar, AV requirements, keeping peace, etc. It was great training for a career as a wedding planner and boxing referee.

The meetings were held in late afternoon and were followed by cocktails and dinner. This provided the opportunity for office and plant management to build rapport and to become a team. In fact, the meetings were more about 200 stressed guys getting drunk and even occasionally duking it out.

During the meetings I served as "cow hand," making sure the herd was quiet during the monotonous presentations and controlling the inevitable stampede to the bar. I learned to sense when the herd was getting restless and knew the words "…and so in conclusion" was the clap of thunder that would start the herd moving. I learned not to get in their way lest I be trampled and to get help to turn them if they were about to careen wildly off a cliff. Sometimes I was too late. And if the evening ended without a belligerent shouting match or fistfight, we felt rapport had been improved.

I found a partial remedy for my own stress in two—three—or four trips to the bar. I worried about it, but didn't feel so bad about it. This became a dangerous habit in time.

I admired our Plant Manager for trying to bring an enlightened style of management to our business. I think he was ahead of his time, but someone had to be first to step off the cliff. For us it became 'our time,' and to a large degree, it worked.

Chapter 35.
Les' Dream—A Nightmare

Spring came, and the plant was up and running without incident. I found enough bodies to fill all the cracks without recruiting at the State Mental Hospital. Turnover was high, especially in the processing area where the horse guts and chicken heads were ground up and cooked in the huge gloppita-glop machines. The resulting discharge was a brownish blue, blah, diarrhea-looking slurry with a smell that made your eyes water. But after adding a little deodorant and a little red dye, the goop was converted into an eye-appealing, edible state for dog and man and sent oozing down a tangle of tubes to spotless packaging rooms. There it was formed into mouth-watering looking patties and shipped on to your grocer for your dog's gourmet eating pleasure. (Or, in hard times, perhaps for your own.) Gaines Burgers was a raging success, and I was proud of myself.

Things were going well enough to feel cautiously confident and optimistic. Maybe I could do this thing! I just needed a little more time to adjust.

But there was no more time.

Les wanted a baby.

It was following the 1966 first quarter's business review/team building session and bacchanal that Les set her dream in motion. It's hard to recall clearly the night's events through the haze of semi-drunken stupor. But this night left one or two clear images:

I arrived home very late at about five Manhattans past a few beers. I assumed Les was already in bed asleep, considering the hour. Exhausted and a little more than half bagged, I struggled to bed and found—Surprise!—Les was not asleep—not at all. And she was intent on playing. Her game required my full cooperation. "The spirit is willing but the flesh is weak" was apropos of the moment. Les was not to be deterred. She would have her way. She kissed and coaxed and fooled around, and I was ravished.

Oh, the shame of it!

Her thermometer said it was time. Les would have her baby. About two months after succumbing to my beautiful Les' charms, I came home one evening and found a small, gift-wrapped package with my nickname, "Brigs," sitting on my dresser. Les appeared in the doorway smiling. I smiled back with a puzzled look on my face, feeling guilty for not having a gift for her too—embarrassed that she bought me something for some special reason (I had no idea what). I methodically removed the gift-wrap and read the two words on the cover of the tiny box inside: Ear Stopples. I thought, *What are ear stopples and why would Les consider them something I would like to have?* It took 3 or 4 seconds for the chain to catch on the crank. Ear plugs! We were pregnant! We were going to have a baby! The doctor said late November or early December. I was happy, and I was my old self again; happy just thinking about all the things I could worry about now.

We were excited! But I wasn't sure. *Is this the end of our freedom? What kind of father will I be? What if I lose my job?*

It'll Be Okay In The Morning

Can I support a family? Do I want to have to support a family? Is this too soon? I didn't answer.

We needed to share the excitement of our baby with our families. We made the phone calls, hoping the excitement would be shared, forgetting the kind of parents we had; forgetting why we didn't miss them.

With the exception of my dad, who was always excited to hear from anyone about anything, God bless him, the other three parents were urbane, aloof about things most people would find exciting. My mother's response to the news was her usual, simple, detached "That's nice, Dear." The same "That's nice, Dear," she gave Dad the Christmases he gave her the diamond Hamilton watch and the fur coat.

Les' parents had always treated her like a visitor in their home. A welcome visitor, certainly, but a visitor—an outsider—someone who was stopping by for a while but not of significant or lasting importance in *their* life together. She was used to being left out—a fifth wheel. Her dad gave her handshakes instead of hugs. So, when she called and announced the news to her mother, we were pleasantly surprised with her mother's sincere elation. She told us she and Charles would come and visit for Thanksgiving, before the baby was born.

The months passed, and Thanksgiving arrived along with the Charles and Helen.

I didn't like my father-in-law, nor did he care for me. We both tried not to show our mutual dislike, but neither of us played the role very well. Charles ("Don't call me Charlie") was an engineer and thought everyone should be. He was cold and humorless and always involved in his own world, doing what he pleased when he pleased.

I tried hard—too hard—to impress him. Overly gregarious and engaging to the point of obsequious nausea, I kept tripping over my tongue. Charles was reclusive, standoffish. It must have always rankled him when I ignored his hand and instead embraced him when we greeted each other. I convinced myself it was just a pleasantly disarming thing to do, but now I'm sure I really knew it pissed him off.

The Urbans arrived late on Wednesday, and we planned a quiet Thanksgiving Day with a very brief tour of Kankakee, followed by our Thanksgiving dinner.

The time and the tour went well. Les and her mother struggled with the turkey and the trimmings in the tiny kitchen while I struggled to carry on a conversation with the "turkey" in the living room.

Dinner was served. As she has done everything in her life, Les bent over backwards to make sure things were perfect: china and crystal and her parent's favorite creamed onions, always served on Thanksgiving Day, and *only* on Thanksgiving Day. We had almost finished when Les excused herself to go the bathroom. Some time passed and I wondered why she hadn't returned as I carried on the awkward conversation. She returned to the table. "Brian, can I see you for a minute?" She motioned to me. Something was wrong.

She took me aside and said, "I'm bleeding." She went on to try and be reassuring, "These things are not that uncommon, but I think we should call the doctor." I tried to calm myself and called while Les told her parents. The doctor was mildly reassuring but told us to get to the hospital right away. He would meet us there.

It'll Be Okay In The Morning

It would be all right. I kept telling myself to hold back panic. Remarkably, unbelievably, Les' parents said they would remain at the house and that we should call to keep them posted—like some news service.

We didn't speak much on the way to the hospital. What few words were exchanged were weak reassurances that all would be fine. "The doctors told us the baby is very healthy...Even if there is a problem, the baby is almost full term and they can take it by Caesarean...We'll just have our baby a little earlier." I tried to reassure Les, but my insincerity screamed through.

We arrived at the hospital at about 8:00 pm. There was no waiting. The doctor was already there. I was bruskly shuttled off to a waiting room. The doctors immediately took Les away. Any show of reassurance had gone. My fears for Les and the baby skyrocketed out of control as I watched them go.

How much time passed? Minutes? Hours? I paced in the small room, alone. I wrung my hands and prayed, prayed hard, promising God all kinds of quid pro quos. I knew that if I could just worry hard enough, things would be okay.

What's keeping them? Where are they? I thought. *It's going to be okay. They'll come and tell me the baby is born—that I'm a father and Les is doing fine.* The door of the waiting room slowly swung open, and the doctor entered. He wasn't smiling. My heart was going to burst from my chest. *How bad could it be?*

"Mr.—" (he struggled with Cosacchi), "your wife is fine. She's not in any danger." I was not relieved. I knew Part B was coming from the way he said Part A. And I knew he wanted me to know.

He went on, "—but, I'm afraid I have to tell you that the baby is not doing well and will probably not survive. There is nothing we can do." He went on to explain that Les had experienced an abruptio placenta, a peeling away of the placenta from the uterine wall, preventing the baby from getting oxygen.

"Does Les know? Can I see her?" I said. I thought, *Can nothing be done—what about my deal with you God? Where are you God?*

The doctor wasn't done. "Mr. Cosacchi, we could take the baby by Caesarean section but even if it did survive, it's been without oxygen for some time now and would certainly be severely handicapped, and Mrs. Cosacchi would have to have any future children by Caesarean. I know it sounds hard, but we would recommend she give birth to your child normally, even though it will be stillborn."

What is this? I thought. *Has the whole world gone completely mad? Give birth to a dead baby? What is this, God, some horrible retribution for my not going to church anymore? Aren't there worse people in the world to pick on?*

It was 3:00 in the morning. I must have nodded affirmation to the doctor's recommendation, assuming Les had also. I went to see her and tried to be strong, but I think she wanted me to cry. She was stoic, but she cried ,and I couldn't console her. Whatever words we exchanged must have been trivial reassurance about the future. "The doctor said we can have other children. He said this would have no impact on getting pregnant again. He said you'd be okay—you'd be—okay." She'd be okay.

I saved what was inside me until I got back to the deathly quiet of the waiting room before I let it all go. And I let it go all over the room. It surged out of me like sorrow's vomit. I banged fists and head against the beige-tiled walls, hurting myself as much as I could stand, then chastising myself for being unable to take any more. I wanted to suffer with Les. I might have wanted to die, but then who would suffer with Les? This was my fault. I should have done something to save our baby. I was a failure—again.

The doctor returned and told me Les had given birth to a beautiful little girl. He asked if I would like to see the baby. I couldn't, nor could Les. He asked if we wanted to give the baby a name. I thought that cruel at the time. "No." I replied. "No name." Sometimes I wish we had. She was part of us. She was our first daughter.

It was morning. I dutifully called our home to tell the Urbans. Helen expressed great sorrow. Charles was working on something. He left the next day. Helen explained his rapid departure. "Charles is a very sensitive person and does not handle sorrow or tragedy very well. You understand." I did not. I didn't know anyone who handled tragedy well. That's why they called it tragedy. He was a thoughtless, self-involved coward schmuck, and I would never be afraid of him again.

Helen stayed a few days with Les. We were grateful. We had no one else. We didn't even have each other. Our marriage survived, but we would never be the same. We would have to get used to living with tragedy.

God didn't like us.

I wasn't with her when she delivered our stillborn daughter. I didn't go through the labor with her except to visit and hold her hand now and then. I was not able then and will never be able to imagine the unbelievable desperation and sorrow that must have overwhelmed my beautiful wife.

    Les needed to grieve. I needed to move on. We grieved and moved on.

Chapter 36.
Our First Home

After the baby died, it took time to find life again—to smile and feel it—to acknowledge sunshine. Les needed time to grieve and physically recover. I didn't understand. I was lost in grief and feelings of guilt that there must have been something I could have done to save our baby—something. I kept erasing the idea from my head, but it kept popping back up like bubbles in an oil lamp. It still does, but less often now. We were never the same again—not as individuals—not as a couple, and life didn't get easier.

When the Gaines Burger plant successfully started up, I earned a promotion back to White Plains. We were anxious to go. They only allowed us one trip to find a place to live, so we asked and trusted Charles and Helen to find the best value home they could within commuting distance of White Plains.

The raised ranch on Ashbee Lane in Ridgefield, Connecticut, was very modest but a bargain at $25,500. The street looked like the builder had started at one end, pointed his bull dozer in a straight line, closed his eyes, shifted into gear and knocked down every tree, scraping the front half of every lot clean. So Ashbee Lane with its little ticky-tacky houses looked like a Monopoly board.

A small brook struggled in the back of our lot, eventually surrendering, giving up, exhausted, spreading out to cover a healthy crop of skunk cabbage that thrived in the black muck.

We were nervous and excited. With CharLes' and Helen's imprimatur and encouragement we signed a "save harmless" letter allowing us to move in before the closing and "saving" the owner from further responsibility. We hurried back to the house—**our house**—to get a better feel for our new home. I began my serious exploration, poking my nose here and there totally ignorant, never sure of what I was looking at or for. I looked in the garage, empty except for the jet pump that I was told drew water from our well. Imagine, a well of our very own. I wanted a closer inspection. I wanted to, I had to, learn about my house—MY HOUSE.

The pump sat on a cinder block in the far corner. I moved close enough to study it. I read, "Dayton 1 Horse Power Jet Pump," followed by a long serial number. I reached down to brush away some of the dust. I tapped the small brass metal plate that contained the model number then jumped back, startled as the pump disintegrated into a hundred pieces. *Oh, my God, I broke it!* crossed my mind just before *Oh my God, the save harmless letter!* Instant sweat, soaring blood pressure, racing pulse. *I couldn't have broken it. I just tapped it with my finger,* I repeated and repeated, my voice rising higher each time.

I ran for Les and found her as she was running for me. "The jet pump just fell apart in a thousand pieces," I said just as she was saying, "It looks like every pipe in the house has burst." We stared at each other for a moment, dumbstruck. We didn't want to believe it. It can't be. She went on, "All the base board hot water copper piping, all the plumbing pipes, even the toilet bowl—all cracked or burst."

What'll we do?

She cried. She told me she was pregnant again.

What'll we do?

The following day the realtor intervened on our behalf, and the plumbing was repaired. We moved in, thanking God but now living in a constant state of "wince," waiting for more surprises. It didn't take long.

It rained. And with the rain came a noxious, repugnant odor wafting through the spring air. I investigated and discovered a bubbling spring silently burping its way to the surface in our front yard. A septic spring of reeking, putrid, malodorous fluid leaching out of our septic fields; spreading out, greening our lawn. When we flushed a toilet, the disgusting effluent would gurgle up all the stronger, and inside the house the basement toilet would sometimes back up and overflow onto the tiled floor.

"What will we do now?" We were repeating the question so often it could have become our motto. We might have put it on our crest, our coat of arms. *O Que Imos Facer!* It could be our morning salutation and bedtime valediction. It could be etched on our gravestones. " What will we do now?"

We consulted with a septic expert. He said we needed more septic fields. We agreed, and the digging began. And for the next year all the people of Ashbee Lane had an ongoing serial to follow. Like Boston's Big Dig there was always some new exciting machine to watch or a rumor about dinosaur bones or some dead person being found in the trenches.

The first corrective attempt added 110 additional feet of fields to our system and fixed the problem for about a week until it rained. Then they too filled up with the fetid effluent, and it again came bubbling to the surface. Undeterred, we consulted with a second expert, an engineer known throughout Ridgefield and adjoining towns for his magical use of a dowser to find wells, septic fields—anything with water. His answer: a curtain drain. He said it with conviction. He promised it would solve the problem—a 250-foot-long, 6-foot-deep trench across the front of our lawn and around the entire side of our house. He explained that this would catch the water coming from springs and higher elevations across the road. It couldn't fail. We sighed our assent.

Our lawn took on the look of a WWI battlefield; trenches running this way and that, up and down, and crisscross. When the digging ended, the new curtain drain was filled with crushed stone and covered over, leaving nasty scars in what had been a prideful lawn. We were relieved until the first hard rain. It didn't work either.

Chapter 37.
The Job

My new job was Associate Manager of College Recruiting. It involved attracting and hiring the best kids out of the best schools. Our competition was Procter and Gamble, Nestle, Kraft, Kellogg's and other big consumer goods companies.

Getting the job done required some fawning over college placement directors to induce them to recommend us to their kids. We wanted to keep our name in front of the best students like being on top of a Google list and to make sure they signed up for an interview with us at the end of the school year. We plied the directors with favors.

We became a circus sideshow of corporate factotums visiting the campus big top throughout the year, wining and dining the placement officer and key faculty members. We swung high on the trapeze, juggled and clowned around and walked a tight rope of questions. And when it was time to interview, I brought a GF "strong man" with me to ostensibly handle one of the interview schedules, but really to impress everyone that such an important person would take the time to talk to mere students.

For me the visits, the fawning was tedious: shake hands firmly, keep smiling; "What a great job you're doing." Tell them how much we depended on them until my pasted-on smile began to give me cheek cramps.

But the campus visits were refreshing compared to the days of interviewing, watching the clock and telling time by the number of interviews. The kids were great. They always shook hands firmly, kept smiling hard until they began to get cheek cramps and always made some honeyed comment, "What a great company you are," and how much they wanted to work for us—were depending on us.

They came, one after another, from 8:00 until 5:00 or 6:00 every 25 minutes, with five-minute grace periods between to sum up or go to the bathroom. Sometimes there were scheduling errors, and I interviewed as many as seven students at once. Fourteen to thirty kids all trying to impress us that they were among the best and that they really wanted to do "this" work. But most didn't know what "this" work was. Most just wanted to get a job offer, not necessarily to accept the offer but to assure themselves of some job—any job—when they ultimately left the campus womb.

I remembered!

I asked them canned questions and often received canned answers. The best and brightest got past the canned and into the candid. Many knew more about our business than I did. I certainly was not among the best and brightest, but I practiced pretending to be. Still, we got our fair share of those gifted ones.

General Foods was a great company to work for. We valued talent, commitment and vast differences in culture and outlook among the people who worked with us.

Chapter 38.
The Clown Car

In the meantime, over these months, Les' belly grew bigger, and financial pressures pressed down. We needed a second car. I bought a junk heap, rattletrap called a Sunbeam Imp. I loved it because it was unique. Unique things made me feel unique, special, clever. People would notice me and say, "Now isn't he clever? Isn't he unique?" In reality I was a jerk who didn't catch on to why no one else had a Sunbeam Imp. I didn't learn from my two prior experiences with "unique." A 1958 Saab with a two-cycle engine that smoked, fumed and huffed and puffed and died on the Pennsylvania Turnpike, and my disastrous purchase of a Das Kleine Wunder (DKW—a car no one heard of before or since).

My unique little Sunbeam Imp looked a lot like the new Mercedes Smart Car and got 40 miles per gallon. It was eight years old but had only 50,000 miles on it, and the price was right at $500. It was all we could afford—actually more, considering the few thousand we unsuccessfully put into the septic problem, the repayment of a $1500 loan we borrowed from Les' parents and promised to pay back in six months and Les having to soon quit her job.

And once again, "unique" let me down. Less than a month went by before the water pump stopped pumping. It was to be a $500 repair on a $500 car. It was the final pebble on my pile.

My pile came tumbling down. I was furious that they could have sold me this lemon. It wasn't my fault. I was no patsy. I'd show them. I would demand satisfaction. I drove the Imp to the dealer in stages, allowing it to cool every ten miles or so. And each time it cooled, I grew hotter. *Not going to make a fool out of me—not ME!* I stormed into the dealer's showroom. It was a *Mercedes* dealer's showroom. I intended to yell and pound the table and make my demands, but instead I broke down and blubbered like a baby. I begged for mercy. The dealer couldn't stand the blubbering and name-calling. He was embarrassed. All his potential Greenwich customers were looking. It made them uncomfortable watching a grown man cry and curse and blubber. Maybe I should have been embarrassed, but I was beyond embarrassment. The manager glanced furtively about the showroom, acknowledging the knitted eyebrows and disapproving looks with a plastic smile and trying to "shush" me. A faint moustache of sweat broke out on his upper lip. "I'm sure we can work something out, Mr. Kosnovski," he relented, and cut the cost of the repair in half. I was humiliated but felt exonerated. My blubbering was validated.

The septic problem continued for the next year until our plumber offered a simple solution. His solution would never have met with Sierra Club approval, but it was the only solution other than burning the house down and officially making the lot a cesspool.

Chapter 39.
Tara

Hello 1968!

The months flew by. I never saw January coming, what with all the financial pressures, trying to look smart in a new job that was more boring than a Baptist cocktail hour, commuting in a cracker box car that looked like it came from the Ringling Bros. Circus, limping down the highway farting and dropping "turd" parts every now and then, saving bathroom flushes to keep the bubbling artesian septic fountain below ground and watching and worrying about Les and the baby—the baby. Please God, the baby!

January 19, sometime at night I think, Les was full term, so we breathed a little easier when she said it was time. We were calm outside, but inside I was doing flips and hand stands, wishing it was tomorrow and over, please God, without incident. Les did a great job of disguising her own anxiety. You would have thought we were going grocery shopping. We called the doctor, gathered her things and set off for Danbury Hospital. We didn't appear to rush.

I don't recall the check-in or saying goodbye. There must have been a lump in my throat and I must have been yearning to run in that big yellow open meadow I always thought about when things were beyond my control. I waited in the hallway, wandering down to the scale at the far end and masochistically adding to the tension by stepping on it and cursing myself, *186 pounds, you jerk—you fat idiot. That's it! I'm finished!* Whatever that meant.

I paced and sat but don't remember how long, who came to tell me or what they actually said. Something simple like, "Mr. Cosacchi? Mrs. Cosacchi is doing fine and you have a beautiful new baby girl." And all the fears that had been living inside since Baby Number One died, all that extra baggage that must have accounted for twenty of those extra thirty pounds, all that stifled self blame came to the surface and, for the moment, eased a bit.

"Would you like to see your new baby?" She asked. I really wasn't sure, but it would have been indelicate to refuse. I wonder if I would have been the first new father to ever say, "No way! No thanks, I don't want to see it. Maybe some other time."

I must have followed her, though, because the next thing I can recall I was standing in the brightly-lit hospital room, trying to look thrilled and fatherly, but gawking stupidly like Gomer Pyle from the Andy Griffith Show, *Gaawwly!...Shazzam!* I smiled at my beautiful wife propped in her bed. And there, cradled in the crook for her arm, barely visible, only a small portion of her tiny pink face showing, framed by the blanket and little beanie hat, was our Tara. There is no word or expression that can capture the joy I felt for Les. There is no word that can express how I felt because I had never felt whatever that was. I thought of Billy Bigelow in Carousel singing, "My little girl, soft and pink as peaches and cream is she." Imagine, "My little girl." Me a father. Me incompetent, bumbling Brian, a father. I thought, *I'll have to do my best though, so no one will ever know how incompetent I am. I'll have to do my best for my beautiful wife. I'll work very hard and I won't let myself die for a long time.*

I floated to her bedside, leaned over and awkwardly attempted an embrace, fearful of crushing the tiny baby. Les smiled and looked down at Tara. I don't recall that she or

It'll Be Okay In The Morning

I said anything for some time. Then the words I was fearing, "Would you like to hold her?" I didn't, but I did. I needed to demonstrate that mixed-up, vulnerable, macho, awkward side of all men that can hold a baby without killing it. I succeeded. It felt natural. It felt good. Maybe I can do this. Over time I would hold her often. Those days are now only fond memories. Now I thank God for all she was, has been and is to us. Today, I miss her and would like to go back and hold her again.

Chapter 40.
Karin—Our Third Child—Thy Will Be Done

After Tara was born, I was content. But Les wasn't satisfied. She wouldn't rest until she had a second child—a sibling for Tara to share life with—the sibling Les never had. Les grew up lonely, an outsider in her own home. All her life she mistakenly believed the sadness she felt as an only child had to be the same for all only children. She was intent on having a second child.

But God had other plans for us. We must not have heard him when he said, "Hey you! All you get is one." So we didn't really know any better when we flaunted His will.

We tried again, and again Les conceived. We were sure God would grant her unselfish prayer. But this God was the God of Abraham—the old testament God filled with anger, malice, revenge, and retribution. We chose not to hear him yelling, "What's the matter with you? Are you deaf or just stupid? I told you just one! Live with it!" But Les was not to be denied, and I needed her to be happy and feel fulfilled.

And so it came to pass that Les' time was at hand and she cried out, "Ooops, my water broke. Call the doctor and grab the suitcase." And we were off to Danbury Hospital once again, this time with high hopes. Everything had gone well. Les was full term, and the baby was healthy. We had the chutzpah to settle on names and agreed that if it were a little girl, she would be named Karin.

We checked in, and I left Les to the care of the medical staff and retreated to wait. My *yin* and my *yang* began arguing. *She and the baby will be fine. You have nothing to worry about.*

Oh yeah! I've heard that before. We better expect the worst. I hated to hear from old Yang, but my life's experience gave him the edge in the debate. I pushed him aside and waited.

Time passed quickly and soon the nurse Herald arrived. She brought glad tidings of the birth of a beautiful little girl. In my head I added—*who will be named Karin.* I was greatly relieved and muttered to old Yang to get lost.

"Would you like to see your daughter?" the Herald asked. I nodded and smiled, and we walked to the delivery room. The nurse showed me to a table where the little bundle of baby was resting. She drew back the soft blanket from Karin's face and commented. "Isn't she beautiful?" I agreed and felt like crying. But there was something else. Something just a little disturbing about the way she looked. I said something to the nurse, but she smiled and directed my attention to a color chart on the wall. The chart showed various degrees of newborn coloration. But neither the chart nor her condescending, *What do you know!* smile assuaged my concern. I tried to put it aside, chalking it up to fearful conditioning from old Yang. I went to see Les and said nothing of my layman's observation. We were happy. The baby was beautiful. The concern kept gnawing.

I left to go home for some rest and a bite to eat and returned a few hours later. The gnawing feeling came along too. Yang wouldn't leave, *Be prepared for the worst*, he cautioned again. So even before I entered Les' room, I already knew something was terribly wrong. I saw it in the air, felt it, smelled it, tasted it. She wasn't crying, but her face was cold, hard stone. Her whole self was silently screaming. It was clear she was upset and desperately worried. "The baby is cyanotic. She is a blue baby. She's not getting enough oxygen. They don't know why. They aren't sure they can save her." She didn't say it, but she was beseeching me, begging me to fix it. *Please, I need you to fix it. That's what you're here for. You're supposed to fix it. Don't let this baby die too.* She didn't say it, but I felt blame for our first baby's death, and now I would be to blame if Karin died. I had to save our baby.

I hugged her. I felt like saying, *I'll do what I can*. But it sounded gutless, weak, hollow. So I said nothing. I was already running out the door to find the doctor to tell him to save our baby, to save our Karin. I found myself wishing we hadn't given her a name because, if she died, we would have to remember her. She had a name.

I tracked down Dr. Prince in the hallway outside the nursery. Through the window I could see our baby Karin in an incubator, her tiny chest heaving up and down laboring to catch enough breath to live a little longer.

The doctor was struggling too, trying to maneuver a mobile x-ray machine into the nursery. It wasn't meant for the nursery. They were not prepared for situations like this. Dr. Prince was visibly upset. His fat body was perspiring, trying to swivel the awkward equipment through the barely big enough door.

He stopped for a moment to tell me what I already knew. "We're not sure what's causing your baby's breathing difficulties, an obstruction of some kind—a problem with her blood—her lungs." And then the line that always signaled the worst was about to happen; "But let me assure you Mr. Cosacchi, we're doing all we can—we're doing everything possible." I asked the obvious question, "Is there anything—anyone else—who can help?" He repeated the obvious answer, "We're doing everything possible." Then he dismissed me with; "We'll send for you as soon as we know something." I told him I'd wait in the lounge and the paranoid, self-deprecation began, *You stupid son of a bitch, you stupid idiot, you worthless weakling. You should have insisted on more doctors, better doctors, specialists. You didn't.* I waited, patient and trusting and praying, "God, please save our baby." I didn't realize God was responsible. "Thy will be done."

Time passed slowly, a nightmare relived. After several hours Dr. Prince stepped through the door. I knew even before he said a word, even before I read his expression. Our baby was dead. We went to tell Les. We didn't have to. She cried.

We sank into a miserable silence pit, but deeper this time. No family, no support group, no one to say how sorry they were. Just the two of us, individually groveling in guilt and anger. It piled up high like driftwood and garbage on a beach at spring tide. It could never all be carried back to sea. It would leave a stain and a stink. And God said, "See, I told you not to do that! I warned you. I told you so. Maybe now you'll listen."

We didn't want to hear. We didn't care about God. And remarkably, incredibly, Les was still undeterred. She would have her second child. God and the world be damned. And God fumed. We pushed Him too far. He would teach us a lesson. He would show us who was boss. We would learn that when it comes to inflicting pain and misery, God was just warming up.

Chapter 41.
Captains (not so) Courageous

After a year in college recruiting and a promotion to wage and salary administration, I had to admit that Personnel didn't have much to do with helping people. It seemed that Personnel's function was to justify senior management's decisions. Sycophants! Corporate Whores! But sales people seemed like regular, down-to-earth folks, and I thought I could put the two together Sales and Personnel and become a Sales Personnel Manager.

So I wangled my way into field sales for a couple of years to qualify and become accepted into their brotherhood. I returned to the corporate mausoleum into the newly created position of Region Sales Personnel Manager. It was all I hoped for encompassing the whole HR bag: recruiting, employment, salary administration, labor relations, training and development, minority affairs, and lots of management counseling. I was helping people. It was a great job, and it had its perquisites.

We were frequently invited to national sales meetings to coach and train sales managers, and we used the opportunities to have fun and blow off steam.

On one occasion the five region personnel managers attended an annual Post Division sales meeting at the Hilton Hotel and Resort in Port St. Lucie, Florida. Everyone had a free afternoon. The list of fun activities to choose from rivaled Club Med. Most of our group picked mundane golf or tennis. But my friend Bart Vaughn and I decided we would try something different; sailing in the Port St. Lucie Sound. Neither of us had very much sailing experience, but the waters were calm. It was only two or three miles across, and we were sure we would have no trouble with a simple Sail Fish—a flat board with a sail, dagger board and a rudder.

We hurried down to the marina. When asked whether we had sailing experience we answered honestly, "Some." That was enough for the marina clerk who checked us out.

He showed us to our boat, and, like a couple of giddy kids, we pushed off, aiming our little craft out and across the sound. But problems began immediately. The boat didn't want to go in the direction we pointed it and instead veered off to the left. The little cove we were leaving was covered with dozens of scattered stanchions protruding 10 or 12 feet out the water. And all along the perimeter, quietly sitting, were dozens of extravagant, pretentious pleasure boats: Hatteras, Egg Harbor, Burton, some measuring 70 feet or more. There was no direct way out of the cove, and we had to maneuver carefully.

A strong following wind almost picked us up, yanking the sail forward and perpendicular to the hull of the boat. We lurched forward, laughing nervously, and began to doubt our skill. I hung on to the tiller, but I was unaccustomed to pushing and pulling in the opposite direction from which I intended to go. Bart held on to the sheet and had to pull it in quickly or have the sail smash into one of the barnacle-covered obstacles. As he pulled in on the sail, he changed our direction, and we headed full speed for a beautiful 70 ft. Hatteras yacht sitting peacefully, minding its own privileged business. There was panicked silence until the full force of the little boat smashed against the side of the luxurious yacht. The hollow "thud" resounded around the little cove, and a scream peeled out of the bowels of the yacht, followed by an hysterical little man scrambling from below decks running forward and screaming, "Get away, get away!" We did our best, but the force of the wind and our lack of experience caused our little boat to repeatedly bash up against the Hatteras's beautiful hull before we could free ourselves. The little man was beside himself as he hung over the edge of the yacht chanting in full voice, "Get away, get away!"

Finally we were free and sailing in the opposite direction across the cove. We were working very hard, having no idea what we were doing, and we were getting irritated with each other, discovering our respective incompetence. Then smack, crunch! We crashed again, this time into one of the many barnacle-covered stanchions. I tried to push off several times and finally succeeded, only to be left behind as the boat slipped away from beneath me, leaving me stranded in the middle of the marina, arms and legs wrapped around the pole. Bart sailed off alone toward the other side of the cove. The barnacles cut into my legs, and the embarrassment of looking like a monkey on a stick cut even deeper in to my pride.

Somehow Bart got the damn boat turned around and headed back for me. But he couldn't stop, and I leaped on as he flew by, heading back toward the Hatteras with the little man now standing guard on bow, still screaming and waving, "Keep away, keep away!" I grabbed the tiller from Bart and pushed, hoping and betting we would go the right way. The boat turned sharply to starboard, the sail swung out and we were off into the open water, sailing briskly toward the deserted far shore 2 miles away.

With renewed confidence we began to master our tasks. With me at the tiller and Bart holding the sheet, we cruised along with the following wind pushing us in front of the little waves that added a bit of roller coaster to our ride. But when I looked back at those same waves breaking behind, I had an uneasy feeling about our return.

The far side of the little sound raced toward us. The Sail Fish bumped up against a waiting hummock. The stiff breeze pushed us gently broadside against the mangroves and we sat and rested. We laughed at each other. We laughed at the little man yelling and screaming. We laughed at the Hatteras we had torpedoed. We laughed at the sight of me with my arms and legs wrapped around that pole and we rested. But in the back of my mind I was thinking, "I wonder how hard it will be to get back?"

"Well, I guess we better get started." Bart nodded. I pushed the boat off the tangled mangrove roots, but it just bumped back again. We tried again and again, but each time the wind caught the sail and sent us back. Finally I eased myself over the side. I touched bottom about waste deep and sank a foot or so into the muck. Bart pulled up the dagger board and passed me the rope, and I towed us far enough from shore to let the sail out and gain a little momentum.

We gained speed and felt relief as we skimmed along. We learned quickly how to turn around, and we sailed back and forth across the wind for a time until we realized we weren't getting very far. At the rate we were going, it would take several hours to get back. We decided we had to go faster and deduced that it was the dagger board that was slowing us down. We pulled it up, and sure enough, we gained speed immediately.

It'll Be Okay In The Morning

Again it didn't take long for us to realize we hadn't moved any closer to home. In fact we were moving backwards, just sliding back and forth on the same line still a mile-and-a-half from the safety of the marina and the screaming little man.

I was getting worried. I could see the newspaper headlines, "Two General Foods managers disappear in St. Lucie Sound. Search ends without hope."

We had to do something. I thought of all the creativity workshops I had conducted and pushed my imagination. I saw Humphrey Bogart pulling the African Queen through the Zambezi marsh. "I'll tow us." Bart didn't object. The sun had burned him to a crisp by now. He was very quiet. I slid into the water, grabbed the rope in one hand and began to paddle. After progressing 5 or 10 yards in the first ten minutes with waves breaking over my head, swallowing quantities of the St. Lucie Sound, my little creative voice inside said, *Are you nuts? You're going to drown.* I had to agree and climbed back on board. We let the wind jibe the sail, and we sat. It was getting late. We forced a pathetic laugh at our predicament. Surely they would begin to look for us and send help. Wouldn't they?

"What's that sound?" My oversized ears scanned the surroundings. Hmmm, Whirrrrrr, Buzzzzz. A boat! It's a boat. Miracle of miracles, a half mile away speeding along a line parallel to our own—a boat! There it was, our salvation, bouncing off the waves. If we could only signal. If they could only know we were in trouble. I grabbed the dagger board and stood up careful not to fall and capsize. The little waves were bigger now and splashed over the bow. I began waving the dagger board. I remembered seeing movies of people shipwrecked and marooned, waving and yelling at ships far off or at planes several thousand feet above and thinking, *How stupid. Maybe, if you're very lucky, they might see you but they could never in a million years hear you.*

Nonetheless I started yelling, "Help! Help!" and continued waving the dagger board. Our Great Wet Hope was still far away, but it looked as if they were passing. We're lost. No—they were turning. We're saved. No they're passing. We're lost. No. They *were* turning. We're saved!

Bart was quiet. He smiled. His lips cracked. The 18-foot runabout pulled alongside. "You alright?" We smiled weakly, meekly and nodded. "Toss me your line." We gratefully complied. We were dragged slowly, a willing dog on a tight leash as our master "put-putted" us back to safety; beaten, whipped, looking forward to getting it all behind us. When we checked in, a group of sight-seers who had just returned from a pontoon boat excursion were talking animatedly about the fourteen-foot alligator they had seen on the other side of the sound—where we had just come from. Bart and I just looked at each other.

We didn't tell anyone the whole story of our adventure, pride being what it is. We were glad to be back.

Post script:
The gremlin in me couldn't resist. Two weeks later Bart received a phone call from a man who said he was an insurance investigator representing a gentleman who owned a 70-foot. Hatteras. He said he was looking for the individuals who caused $30,000 of damage to his client's boat.

I didn't tell Bart it was a practical joke for more than a month. He laughs about it now, but I don't think he ever forgave me.

Chapter 42.
Finally, A Second Child

Life was good at home and on the job. Things were going well.

Tara was a delight, a perfect little girl with something new and exciting to share with Dad every day; adorable, curious, always busy and loveable. She had been that way ever since the moment she popped out of her mom.

We decided to cash in on the real estate market. The house problem on Ashbee Lane had finally been fixed. I found an exciting lot behind some huge boulders in the town of Newtown. Charles, Les' father, helped us design a beautiful contemporary home.

The sadness of the tragedy of losing Karin faded, but not Les' resolve to have another child. Maybe if our Tara hadn't lived, or if she had been born severely physically or mentally disadvantaged, maybe then we would have given up. Maybe if we couldn't bring a child into this world at all we would have accepted that God had other plans for us, or that maybe He just thought we would never be good enough parents.

But Tara lived. And Tara was perfect. The death of our first baby, who never had a birth certificate but might have been named Dorian, and then the tragedy our third child, Karin, left me with doubts. But Tara made Leslie all the more determined to have a second child. Tara would not grow up alone!

Getting pregnant was a bit of a problem, trying so quickly after the birth of our third baby, but after around nine months we again were pregnant. The explosion of passion and the ecstasy of the moment obscured worries about tomorrow, clouded memories about yesterday—numbed fear.

So Les looked forward to her fourth child. And to minimize any risk of failure we placed our faith in the hands of the best obstetrician and the best hospital on the East coast: Dr. Patrick Duff and the Yale New Haven Hospital. These medical magicians would take on the Almighty and facilitate the welcome of the Cosacchi's second whole, living, healthy child into this world.

The months passed, anxiety built and the day arrived. We drove the thirty-five miles to the hospital with calm, almost jubilant euphoria. All had gone well again in this pregnancy. The doctor had told us that the chances of a third birth anomaly were astronomical.

The staff and hospital at Yale reeked of *professional*. We smiled, lulled into comfort, confidence—peace of mind. I was shamed into being with Les in the delivery room to watch the birth by the nurse-midwife. I was reluctant, fearing I might slow the process down by vomiting or passing out.

The delivery room was crammed with 11 people: everyone standing at the ready. I thought we might hear a fanfare and they all might salute or offer a round of applause as Dr. Duff entered.

The show began. All the people began hustling about. Dr. Duff was the center of attention even though Les was the star of the show. He looked up, raised his rubber gloved

It'll Be Okay In The Morning

hands in the air as if to offer a sacrifice or give the orchestra a down beat. Then he looked down and began to work in earnest. He disappeared under the tasteful white drape that hung from Les' knees. It only took a moment. Dr. Duff reappeared like a magician pulling a rabbit from a hat. He held little Christopher in the air, and the little rabbit began to cry. So did Les. So did I, and the thought of vomiting never returned. We were happy. We had a son—a healthy, strong son. Maybe the All Merciful had relented.

Les had a day or two to enjoy her new Christopher Charles Cosacchi before having to pack him off to the routine of our new life together. I came to visit and be with them each day. Finally, graduation day! Smiles and hand shakes and thanks all around from the mother and father.

As innocent infant Christopher lay on the hospital bed looking up, I looked down and smiled, then stopped. *But wait, what's this?* I said to myself. I tried to calm myself. *Stop looking for things*, I chastened myself. *He's been here for days. It's not possible they would have missed anything. But go ahead, make a fool of yourself. Better to ask now and get reassured than to leave here with the question.*

So, feeling a little foolish and with confidence and a light heart, just to calm myself, I smiled to Dr. Duff. "Ya know, I'm sort of a worry wart, Doc, after all we've been through. So excuse my question, but do Christopher's eyes look a little different to you?"

I had expected Dr. Duff to laugh and dismiss my foolish fear out of hand with some simple explanation. He didn't. I took a deep breath and held it. Les heard the question and caught the non-committal response.

Dr. Duff looked down at the baby. Indeed his eyes were different. Then, trying to assuage our fears and at the same time prepare them for some new tragedy, he said, "Well, I guess we better check it out." He lifted little Christopher, "Be back as soon as I can." He left.

We avoided looking at each other. There was that sinking feeling. Dr. Duff could take his time. We both knew. The astronomical possibility was a reality. We didn't embrace. We didn't cry. We didn't support each other, lie and tell each other, "It'll be okay." We had been here before.

How long was it before Dr. Duff returned? Ten minutes? An hour? We wished he'd never return. We wished we could turn the clock back. Now I asked God, "Please save my son."

He returned. "I'm afraid your son's vision is severely impaired. We can't really tell how severe his vision loss is. He may have some vision, but there is clearly substantial loss."

I choked back tears. Doctor Duff returned my son to my arms. I said to myself, "He's my son. It's up to me. I'll make it all right. He'll have whatever he needs." I believed I could do it. I believed it was up to me.

I thought of Les and realized there was no consolation I could offer her. She always pushed me away in tragedy and suffered alone. Nothing I could do could ease her pain. I thought, *Please God, help us.*

On the drive home we thought about how we would tell Tara. Over the months we had sold her on the great fun she would have with the new baby. Now she was waiting at home, all excited, anticipating the baby brother her Mom had promised. Telling her that her baby brother couldn't see was going to be a difficult thing.

So on March 3, 1972, the beginning of our crusade to raise a legally blind son began. We made a few good decisions along the way and a few serious mistakes.

We contacted the Connecticut State Services for the Blind. They were helpful and reassuring. And we watched him grow. He was adorable. His eyes were dark like Little Orphan Annie's. They made him look strangely endearing, especially when they were wrapped in his glorious ear-to-ear smile. He didn't know what it was not to see.

We loved to listen to his "steamroller" laugh. It started as a little giggle in the back of his throat and wound up in a crescendo that shook his whole little body—a laugh so infectious we began to laugh with him. He couldn't see well, but he was strong, and he seemed happy. I swore I'd help him become all he could be. He was my son. I was responsible. He would have what he needed to be successful and happy. Maybe he would be a professor or a lawyer or a businessman, maybe someone who could help others. He'd be okay- my son!

Chapter 43.
Getting On With Life

So Les got her wish—a second child. But I thought God made his point. "You want a second child that bad? Then I know you'll take good care of this one."

Our two children grew up. Chris tried so very hard to be *normal*. He didn't want to be different from the other kids and had no one to look to to be *like*. He tried so hard for so long, but, over time, we watched his spirit soften. The jibes and picking and bullying from other children left him with a huge chip on his shoulder. He would have mountains to climb. His cup of courage emptied. I felt helpless. I couldn't fix it for him. I was responsible. I was his dad.

Tara was always motivated. She has some built-in generator. From the time she popped out of her Mom, she's been busy doing good things. Busy, busy, busy! Like her Mom, 24/7. Industrious, successful, delightful and thoughtful of others. She soared: President of her eighth grade class, her high school class, National Honor Society, Notre Dame Scholarship, successful in business and in motherhood and on and on. While I take tremendous pride in her, her achievements are her own. I don't think she ever needed encouragement. What applause we gave was just icing on the cake.

Her success may have made it more difficult for Chris.

In 1971, before Christopher was born, we had sold our money pit in Ridgefield and moved to the more civilized town of Newtown, Connecticut. We, or rather Les, built a beautiful home designed by Les' dad. It was our secret contemporary hideaway tucked behind a wall of thirty-foot boulders. My commute increased to 102 miles round trip each day, but we loved our home, and Newtown seemed to be a better place to raise a family. But after a few years I wanted more. My dream was a year-round home on beautiful Lake Candlewood north of Danbury where we could swim and water ski and fish and ice skate and sail. I found a magnificent lot in the tiny town of Sherman, overlooking the lake with a view to take your breath away. The mountains came right down to the water, making a dramatic presentation. No one else thought a house could be built on the lot. But we did.

Again Les was the general contractor and did a marvelous job, and we had a home that could be the envy of millionaires. The sun rising in the east caromed off the water, exploding the morning sun into our bedrooms; and at night the moon and stars reflected so brilliantly on the still lake that it was hard to distinguish the reflection from the reality.

My commute increased again, but it was worth it. I was traveling more and commuting less, and General Foods began *early out* on Fridays so we had longer weekends on the lake. Our home was idyllic!

However, when it came to raising our son, the price may have been too high. We will never know how things might have turned out had we stayed in Newtown. There is reason for me to place substantial blame on myself for the nightmare that has been his life—and consequently ours.

Sherman was a very small town. The school was kindergarten through eighth grade and had only a couple of hundred children attending. Resources to help Christopher were limited. When he began school we mainstreamed him. Everyone thought he could keep up with the other kids with a little extra help. Academically Chris did fine for the first few years.

But we did not think enough about how Chris would be accepted by his peers. What would it be like being a visually impaired kid among all fully sighted children? What activities could he participate in? As he grew, the questions became problems. The biggest problem by far was the cruelty of other children. It made me angry and broke my heart that he had to endure so much. He so much wanted to be like all the other children.

One day when he was eight or nine, he said, "Dad, I want to play little league. I can do it. I know I can." I tried to dissuade him, but he was resolute. He had to find out for himself. We had to let him try. I went to his first team practice and he seemed to be doing okay. If the ball came in his direction, much of the time he would eventually see it. But after his second practice his coach suggested I come and watch. The boys were warming up by tossing a ball back and forth about six or seven feet away from each other. Chris was paired with a friend. I watched, and my heart sank as I watched Chris struggle to try and catch the ball. It bounced off his chest, his shoulder, his permanently outstretched glove. He wanted so desperately to be normal. When batting practice began, the coach placed Chris in the safest position: right field. I wandered out with him and stood behind him to give encouragement as the first batter stood at the plate. The batter swung and connected; a line drive flew over the first baseman's head directly toward Chris. Had I not reached my hand out in front of his face to stop the ball, Chris might have taken the full force of that line drive somewhere on his nose or cheek. My being there, the ball being hit so directly at Chris is almost unbelievable—far beyond coincidence. There would be other times in Chris' life where God gave us a break. I hope some day we understand why.

Baseball was not to be. We tried soccer. The ball was bigger, easier to see, and for eight or nine year-olds soccer is just a knot of children pushing a ball around a big field. Still, some parents were extremely competitive, Chris' coach being one. Even though the rules stipulated that every child should play equal time, it was clear the coach would not apply this rule to Chris. I approached the coach, who promptly lost his temper and let me know how obligated I was to him for taking Chris on his team at all. (In fact Chris was assigned to the team and the coach had nothing to do with it.) Nonetheless, Chris received more play time. But it became clear he could not keep up with the other boys, and he soon became the brunt of jibes and name-calling. "Hey, Blindie, can't ya see the ball?" "Blindie" became his unwelcome nickname.

Maybe if we had stayed in Newtown there would have been enough other children so Chris might have made a few more friends. Maybe the kids in Newtown would not have been so cruel.

There were sparks of hope along the way. Chris began playing the drums almost out of the womb. It became a talent, a diversion and a source of pride for him.

When he was ten he joined The New Fairfield Sparklers Drum Corps. He was good at it. He was proud of himself.

We bought him an All Terrain Vehicle and let him ride it around our little private community. It was illegal but most of the residents didn't mind. Then we got a second ATV so he could ride with a friend.

It'll Be Okay In The Morning

I bought a ski boat, and when Chris got over his initial fear of the water, he learned to water ski. We spent Sunday mornings on the pristine lake skiing with Dunkin Donuts and our neighbors. In the early morning, before any other boat traffic stirred up the lake, it was like glass. Our slalom skis cut through the water, making a whooshing sound and leaving a 15-foot rooster tail behind as we cut back and forth across the boat's wake. Chris excelled and learned to ski barefoot. In his early teens he was good enough to compete in a couple of local events. We sent him to Florida for lessons with a professional. He was doing well. He was proud of himself.

But the harassment never let up, and the chip on Chris' shoulder grew bigger each year. I felt helpless, frustrated and angry.

Chapter 44.
Going Over The Top

My frustration and anger came to a head when Chris was in his last year (eighth grade) at The Sherman School. It was Halloween Night, and Chris went Trick or Treating with a friend.

At 9:00 he returned home holding his head. He asked if we could see any of his hair missing. We laughed while we asked what he meant. He went on, " Well, Jason was spraying Nair on kids so they would lose their hair."

You might have heard my mind snap. "Do you have any idea what might have happened if that stuff got in your eye? Is that kid nuts to be spraying that stuff?"

"There's got to be an end to this," I snorted and headed for the garage, not having any idea what I was going to do. I began driving up and down the short steep hills of our small community in my VW Beatle looking for Jason. *When I catch that kid I'm going to...I'll...*but there was no conclusion. What would I do if I found him? Deep down I may have been praying I wouldn't find him. But I did. I pulled my VW Beatle up next to him, rolled down my window, "Jason?" He smiled and nodded in affirmative.

"Have you been spraying kids with Nair? Did you spray Chris Cosacchi with Nair? Do you know what might have happened if you sprayed that in his eyes? Do you know how stupid that was?" These were not questions, and I didn't look for any answers!

His smile disappeared.

"Get in the car." I said. "GET IN THE CAR!" He hesitated, and I jumped out of the car, grabbed his 100-pound, 14-year-old body and stuffed him in the back seat of the Beatle, not knowing what I would do next.

I drove home to our house, herded Jason up the garage steps into our kitchen and sat him in one of the canvas back bar stools. Les was aghast. "What are you doing? Why did you bring him here? What are you going to do? Brian, calm down."

"Don't you move," I told him.

I ran to the bathroom, dug out the electric hair clippers and returned. The boy was obviously frightened. The clippers hummed and buzzed. I clipped clumps of hair here and there. Then I packed him back in the Beatle and drove him home..

On the way the fog cleared "What have I done? I must be nuts!" I dropped him off without a word to his parents, leaving it for him to explain and fearful that his parents would take a pound of flesh.

The next morning our local resident State Policeman, Ralph, knocked on the door. He knew us. But then he knew everyone in the town of 2,000. And we knew him. Had it been another town—a different family—I would have certainly gone to jail. I received a threat and a lecture and a word or two of, "I understand...I don't blame you for being angry. But you can't take the law into your own hands." That was the end of it. Jason's family never mentioned it and was always cordial. I had been a jerk and was lucky not to have gone to jail. I wanted to save and protect my son. It has taken me years to admit I cannot save nor protect him. But I still try. It's like trying to help a little old lady across the street when she doesn't want to go. It takes a long time, and there's no satisfaction in getting her there because she will just go right back.

Chapter 45.
Sailing on Lake Candlewood

General Foods had early-out Friday beginning in the summer of 1978. We worked an hour longer Monday through Thursday and then bolted from our cages at high noon on Friday. I raced from the building, afraid my boss would decide to invite me along for one of his infamous three-hour liquid lunches. My old reliable VW Beetle waited impatiently in the parking lot, anxious to get on the road and beat the weekend traffic from the city.

I hopped into old Betsy, and we were off, galloping up Interstate 684, 50 miles to our private little slice of heaven—our year-round resort on Lake Candlewood. I approached home along the hillside on Route 39. And, from several hundred feet above, I looked down on Lake Candlewood—a spectacular view—the green foothills of the Berkshire Mountains cascading down to the shimmering waters of the lake. And on this day, even from 600 feet above, I could see a whistling wind whipping the waters, painting the lake with white accents. My heart skipped, and I rushed a little faster, anxious to get home—excited to try my new toy.

Only the week before I had purchased an Aqua Cat, a cheap, poor-man's Hobie Cat—Hobie Cats being the standard in performance catamaran sailing. My little Aqua Cat had no boom, just a sail and a sheet rigged to a fourteen foot mast. Its pontoons were fat and clumsy and hard to turn. It had a large Styrofoam ball at the top of the mast to help keep it from going *turtle*—that is turning 180 upside down—should it ever capsize. And I found it did **that** quite easily. But it was fun to sail, and I could get it up on one rail and cruise along pretending it was a Hobie. On this day, with this wind, it would be a Hobie and then some.

The kids were out early from school for some reason on this particular Friday, and I invited them to come along to enjoy the thrill of sailing in a good, strong breeze and to show off a little as Captain Dad. But I insisted both of them wear life jackets. I was not so much concerned about them drowning as I was their getting water in their ears as both recently had tubes inserted to help prevent their frequent ear infections. There were no arguments, and we hurried down the long flight of stone steps to the lake. The kids donned their life jackets. Regretfully, I did not.

We were off quickly as the Aqua "tub" needed no rigging. The wind in our little protected cove was coming from the port stern. I let the sail out, and we covered the quarter mile to the open yawning mouth of the lake in record time. As we reached the end of the cove, I could see the choppy white-capped waves 100 yards off to my left. They were running two to three feet—monsters for our normally placid Candlewood Lake and a possible threat to our little tub. I dismissed the little rush of fear as just excitement, and I prepared to turn to port to catch the full force of the wind and give Chris and Tara a thrilling ride. But even before I moved the tiller, even before I pulled in the sail, the wind hit us a broadside that jerked the sheet from my hand and catapulted all three of us from the canvas trampoline into the roiling chop. There was no time to warn, no time to prepare. Just shock and *Aw, shit.*

I don't think people in these situations really think about dying. At least, at first, it's more a matter of surprise and embarrassment. But it doesn't take long to objectively figure out that embarrassment could wait. For now it really was a question of how to save the kids—how to survive.

The clumsy old tub instantly went turtle. The Styrofoam ball was useless. The wind drove it down so hard it flipped 180 degrees and now pointed to the bottom. All that was left on the surface were the two clumsy pontoons. The uncommonly imposing waves broke over them pushing the Aqua Cat down the lake and the three of us along with it.

The children were terrified. I was terrified. I jerked my head around hoping to discover some other boat—any other boat, but there was none. The kids started screaming and struggling to keep their heads above water, At this point they were only worried about getting water in their ears.

But they soon panicked and started screaming. And I found myself screaming like a lunatic at the top of my lungs, "Be calm—everyone be calm." Who the hell was everyone! But my pleadings were useless, and the children upped the panic ante, trying to climb on top of me, not realizing that I was being run down by a pontoon steam roller—and me the only one of us without a life jacket. I held onto the pontoon that was threatening to roll over me and tried to pull myself up with Christopher virtually sitting on my head. Tara was doing somewhat better controlling her sobs but killing me with an imploring, accusing look that read, *Do something, Dad, You put us here, and you're the Dad. Do something.* I was lost for ideas except to hold on and let the wind push us until we reached shore or could swim to land. With Christopher being only seven, not much of a swimmer, mostly blind and in choppy three-foot waves, the swimming option was very limited.

It had only been minutes. I was tiring, but I had to save us somehow. Maybe a prayer, I thought, and as I thought it, a rope dropped out of the sky.' *Oh my God, I've got to try this prayer thing more often.* The kids saw the rope too, and the screaming ceased as they saw the source of the rope before I did.

I will never understand where he came from or how he got there without me seeing him. It was our neighbor and plumber, Paul Ormiston. To this day I will swear he was dropped from the sky. But who believes in such miracles especially ones that would cast a plumber in a staring role? Nonetheless there he was in his 18-foot Bayliner only 30 feet away. I grabbed the rope, slipped it around the pontoon and we all simply waited as the boat pushed through the waves and settled, marking time.

The rest of the story is simple and undramatic. Paul helped us board. I rested, recovered, reentered the water, and dove the 14 feet down to the top of the mast. I attached the rope, resurfaced and, with Paul's help, righted and recovered the Aqua Tub. How could I ever thank him? He saved our lives that day, and more importantly helped me save at least some face with my children.

This, you may recall, was my second hard sailing lesson, the first being my adventure with my friend Bart Vaughan in Port St. Lucie.

But since this close call I have been a little more cautious—a little afraid to sail—except for the time I almost killed my friend Bob Clark on Lake Travis in Austin, Texas, or the time I nearly crashed the Cal 26 Les and I rented at the Bitter End in Virgin Gorda into the coral reefs. Or the time I nearly tore the bottom out of our rented Robolo 24 off Mosquito Island in the Caribbean. But that's another story and another story and another story.

Chapter 46.
A Skating Adventure with Tara

Our home on the lake was a consolation: rapturous views of sky and water as far as the mind could see; springs, summers and autumns filled with swimming, boating, sailing, water skiing, canoeing, fishing and scuba diving.

But then, winter! And the curtain came crashing down. Silence!

The boats disappeared from the lake along with the leaves from the trees. The whirlwind summer social life with the rich and famous New York weekenders sadly concluded as they headed south to Manhattan and Florida along with the Canadian Geese.

The basement filled with cords of firewood to feed our wood furnace. Weekends were spent finding, hauling, cutting, splitting and stacking to keep the basement full and keep the heating bill down.

And along with the departure of the summer breeze went almost all my opportunities to be remembered by my kids as the strongest, best looking, funniest, daredevil father ever.

The only winter stage was the ice—the six- to twelve-inch-thick frozen lake. Years before, ice boating had been popular on Lake Candlewood. But springs in the lake left the ice dangerously thin in places. A few boats were lost, and ice boating ceased. But in the many community coves along the lake people still enjoyed ice-skating. The ice in the coves was always thick and smooth, undisturbed by wind and springs.

For me, though, skating was a challenge. I didn't learn until I was in my thirties, and then not very well. So, I slipped along gingerly for a time, clumsy, sloppy, erratic. And if I leaned back just a little, my feet would get ahead of me, and I would start to fall backwards. My feet would speed up trying to compensate. faster and faster until they were a blur. My arms spinning backwards to try and regain balance as my renegade feet flew out from under me in a Buster Keaton fall that left me on my back with cracked head and crushed ego. Certainly not an activity to showcase skill and daring for my children.

But one particular morning when the ice was as thick as it had ever been, when it was free of snow, slick and clean and black, Tara and I ventured onto the ice for an extraordinary adventure.

On some previous day I had noticed that when the ice was this slick and when the wind was strong and coming from the north, I could travel for distances without effort by simply standing tall and raising my arms. My body became a sail. I could steer by simply twisting left or right.

This day Tara and I created an adventure we would always remember. I explained our mission: Six miles down the lake was the community of Candlewood Isle. It might take a few hours, and we would have to be extremely careful to avoid ice weakened by springs, but we would undertake the adventure together. I thought, *No father would ever match this feat of daring. I pushed down the other thought, Idiot, you're putting your daughter's life at risk.*

We practiced a few simple moves for a minute or two, and we were off. The end of our safe-haven cove was a quarter mile away. We were there in ten minutes. My second thoughts pricked at my conscience as I looked at the bleak expanse of dark, foreboding desolate, ice that lay beyond the safe haven. The wind from the left where the protected cove joined the open lake whistled low. The voice inside said, *You didn't tell anyone where you were going. Are you nuts to chance this with Tara?* And *Idiot, have you forgotten your famous sailing adventure with your kids, idiot!* But I silenced the voice. I would be the most remembered dad. Tara appeared totally unconcerned, and I would keep her so.

We skated perpendicular to the wind for a moment, its force hitting us broadside. Then we slowly, carefully turned our backs to the wind and raised our arms and began to fly. Ice flying! We practiced slow gentle turns as we floated along on the ice. What fun. I looked at Tara, and her expression was a combination of joy, *I think I've got it*, and fear. *OOPS, maybe not*. My look must have been the same but much more of the *OOOPS maybe not*. After a few minutes I stopped and looked around. The cove was far behind. Ahead there was only the ice and the mountains. We were now in the middle of the lake more than a half mile from either shore. I noticed large cracks in the ice, and the voice rose up again inside. *If something happens, you're dead. There is no one here to help. You're risking your daughter's life.*

Too late, I thought back. *We're committed!* I sailed a little ahead of Tara to look for any springs or thin ice. The cracks in the ice revealed how thick it was. The cracks were most often reassuring. But as we got to the center of the lake, the depth of the ice looked thinner and thinner. Off in the distance to my left I noted an area that glistened and glimmered. Open water.

I slowed our pace. Time passed. I checked the ice depth with frightened frequency. The time being already two hours, I could see Tara was tired.

"How far have we come? How much further? I didn't think it would be this long—this hard." Thank God for the wind. Skating this far would be impossible. I stopped to inspect another crack.

I thought, *What if the ice gets too thin to go further. My God, in this wind we could never make it back, and the shore line is certain to be thawed.* We would have to find a way.

I looked around. Half way. Only half way!

I couldn't estimate the time very well. I looked at my watch. Past noon already. The sky was so dark and gray, it still looked like early morning. It was the kind of day any New Englander could tell you, "Snow is on the way." Tara looked a bit concerned now, and there was little conversation. The fun was wearing off, and we were growing anxious for our destination. We cruised past the Sail Harbor cove. Not a soul.

Just ahead, perhaps three hundred yards, was the last finger of land blocking our view, separating us from our destination another mile or so further on. The finger, with pine trees like dark stiff hairs jutting up toward the gray skies, pointed out toward the middle of the lake—out to where the open water glimmered grimly and beckoned,

It'll Be Okay In The Morning

Come on I dare you. I let the wind continue to push us but relaxed my vigilance in favor of speed, trusting in God and the thickness of the ice, and we hastened our pace skating before the wind to get around and beyond the little peninsula. Once we passed this final obstruction, we would be able to see our destination, Candlewood Isle.

The shimmering open water to my left drew closer, reaching west as we moved on south. I prayed it wouldn't make the turn with us.

I joked and clowned trying to make light of our situation—falling down in mock seriousness, "Oh, we'll never make it," "Ohhhhhhhhhh, I'm so tired," I moaned. Tara laughed, and we started singing as we coasted along. "This old man, he played one. He played nick nack on my drum." Our song disappeared ahead of us blown away in the cold wind that pushed us along.

We were only a hundred yards from the little spit of land that blocked our view of the last mile—our view of where the open water ended—our view of safety.

I was cautiously keeping the shore line a good quarter mile away but pushing us closer to the open water. We swung around the finger tip. The wind died and we slowed to a stop, and there, now less than half a mile away we saw safety, Candlewood Isle. We clearly made out numbers of people skating in the protected cove. The glimmering open water lay ahead of us, but as we skated forward, it grew smaller and smaller and shrank to a ribbon no more than three feet wide. It might as well have been 300. We watched the skaters now less than 50 yards away. We waved. No response.

Wait. Yes, yes, there's someone coming. As they approached, we recognized them. It was the Herbsts. Nancy and Roy and their daughter Danielle. We were saved.

And even as they approached the edge of the freezing ribbon, we heard them yelling, other heads turning, gawking in amazement, "How did you get here? Where did you come from?" "Wow, were you really out there on the lake?"

I smiled, looked at my adoring daughter and very immodestly took the stage and announced, "Yeah, we just skated the eight miles from Deer Run Shores. Nothing to it."

We called home and drank some hot cocoa at the Herbsts', and I promised myself, *No more of these heroic adventures—at least not until summer.*

Chapter 47.
Kent/Saint Howard of Schneider

Chris made it through eighth grade.

Les took a job at the prestigious nearby Kent School Prep School, and while it wasn't part of any plan, we were able to send Chris there as a tuition-free boarder. We were so optimistic about his future: getting away from his tormentors and starting fresh with the prospect of new friends and caring teachers.

"Maybe I'll make some new good friends, Dad." Chris told me with a smile that really told me how tough it was to be "Blindie." Things began well enough, but soon there were red flags: falling grades, altercations with dorm-mates, general unhappiness. We consulted with Chris' teachers and dorm counselor. They all felt Chris was able to do the work but wasn't motivated. Making new friends was not to be.

Then, a few months into the school year, Chris began complaining to Les about discomfort in his eyes. Les reacted faster than a speeding bullet. She took Chris to the local ophthalmologist, but we also consulted with our weekend neighbor, Dr. Howard Schneider. Howard was my weekend tennis partner and a leading ophthalmologist in New York City. He had patients coming from all over the world to his Park Avenue office. There was no one better. His advice was calming, "I'm sure it's nothing to worry about, and I'm sure he (the doctor in Kent) would know this but just be sure, if there is any possibility that this could be a virus—a herpetic virus, under no circumstances should any cortisone medication be used. That would be like pouring gasoline on a fire. But, I'm sure he knows this. It's fundamental."

Les went with Chris to see the local doctor. He examined Chris' eye thoroughly. Les passed along Howard's caution, trying not to be insulting. The doctor acknowledged his understanding, "Of course, Mrs. Cosacchi, that's fundamental. Nonetheless, I'd like to reassure you that this is neither a herpetic virus nor any other kind of virus. It is just a mild bacterial infection and cortisone ointment will clear it up quickly."

We complied, and Chris began to apply the ointment.

Friday came, and Chris was scheduled to come home for the weekend. I arrived at his dorm and made my way to his third floor room. Chris was waiting, sitting on his bed with a wet hand towel on his only semi-good eye.

"It hurts Dad. I can't see very well. If I take off the cloth, it hurts."

I tried to sound calm. But my wheels were spinning—sirens were going off, *Do something! Fix it Asshole!*

"It'll be okay, Chris. Let's go home and get some rest."

Chris stumbled down the stairs to the car holding the moist hand towel to his eye. I couldn't get home fast enough.

I stopped at the first phone booth I could find. Howard—Howard Schneider. *Please God, let him be here.* If worry could make it happen, Howard would be there. The phone began to ring, *Hold your breath. Shut your eyes tight.*

It'll Be Okay In The Morning

Bite your lip. Clench your fists... And it rang. Then an answer: It was his wife, Sandy.

I thought, *okay, don't panic. Keep control.* She put Howard on the phone. I calmly explained and calmly begged him to see Chris. "Bring him right over." He replied without hesitation.

The fifteen-minute trip back to Sherman felt like hours, and when we arrived, Howard was already at our house waiting. He was calm, reassuring. He looked at Chris' eyes with his little flashlight, and after a brief moment he said calmly, "I really can't tell very much with this light. Let me see if we can find someone in Danbury who will let me use his blue light to look at Chris' eyes."

Howard found an ophthalmologist in Danbury who was not only there on this particular Saturday but was someone he had actually taught in school years ago. I asked if he would like some lunch. He calmly but emphatically replied, "Well, I really think we should get Chris on down to Danbury."

We hurried—calmly—to Danbury. Howard greeted his friend and briefly introduced us. He asked me to remain in the waiting room. I waited and twiddled and thought of other things. The examination took only a few minutes. Howard and Chris exited by themselves. Howard smiled a thinly disguised, forced smile. "Well, it looks like we caught this in time. I don't know why that fellow up in Kent would have prescribed cortisone for Chris' eye. It was definitely the wrong thing. So, we have a prescription here that will help. We can stop and get it on the way home. okay?"

I was relieved. "Howard, there is no way I will ever be able to make this up to you. We can pick up the prescription in New Fairfield." Howard responded calmly, "Ahh, no, lets get it right here—right away. No sense in wasting time."

What! I thought. *Right here, right now. That does not sound good.* But I was afraid to ask. "okay. That's fine."

No sooner did we have the prescription in our hands than Howard opened it and applied the ointment to Chris' eye. It was clear this was serious and the outcome somewhat still in doubt.

Chris was stoic. Strong and courageous, and I called him "My Hero" for all he was going through. He had to keep his eyes completely shut for a full week to help healing, and we pulled him out of school from Thanksgiving until classes resumed after New Years. It took several months before his eye totally healed and he was able to see as he had before.

We kept in touch with Howard in New York. The following weekend he looked at Chris' eye again and confided, "Brian, I can tell you now that Chris' cornea was like a crumpled bed sheet, buckled with bumps and ridges. If it had been a couple of hours more—maybe only an hour more—he would have lost much of the remaining vision in that eye. I'm glad I was here. I wasn't supposed to be. You did the right thing."

I did the right thing! I did the right thing! I did the right thing!

We saved what there was of Chris' vision, but the episode was one more pebble on his pile.

Chapter 48.
A Trip To Europe

The Chateau

That same year, 1988, Tara was a sophomore at Notre Dame and was spending the year studying in France. Chris was at Kent so we felt we could break away for a 10-day whirlwind tour of France and Italy. We couldn't pass up the opportunity to be with her, to have her show us around, lead us around, our tour guide—me with my buttons popping. "That's my daughter. *C'est ma fille.*"

Tara met us at the Paris airport. I knew we were in good hands. I thought, "We can just relax and enjoy it. I'm leaving this all up to "Boop" (one of many nicknames conferred on her as a little girl. Others included TuTu, Squagatoomie, Watchachoochie, and Sweet Patootie.)

Tara was able to obtain a free but somewhat Spartan room for our one night stay in Paris. I couldn't figure out the French plumbing: to sit or stand? And I wasn't used to the hand held shower in the open bathtub and gave the walls of the bathroom as much of a shower as I received. Les and I cuddled up on a single cot 'belly to backside'. Tara curled on a mattress on the floor.

We spent just a day in Paris and saw what we could, Sacre Coeur, Montmartre, Eiffel Tower, Versailles, before taking off for Angers where Tara was studying and living with a French family. Tara was like a mother hen looking after us. We met her host family. They were so gracious. We stayed for a wonderful French country dinner of coq au vin. Monsieur Logerais gave us a guided tour of French vineyards. We sampled wines we never heard of and probably will never see on this side of the Atlantic. And we visited magnificent 18th century chateaus—moats and parapets and mirror ponds. Even a black swan here and there floating, drifting gracefully, regally.

Then the big surprise: Tara reserved a room for us in one of those 18th century Chateaus——a romantic interlude for Mom and Dad.

We were greeted in the formal French Provincial entry hall by a shy, young man dressed as a hotel desk clerk, tie and vest—no jacket. Tara spoke with him briefly in French and departed. We were escorted to our room: a four-poster bed, floor-to-ceiling windows looking down at the farmyard and gardens, which hadn't been well attended. Neither had our room. The red plush drapes were worn and threadbare in places. The furniture was a bit rickety, and the canopy over the bed, droopy. The original white color had grown tired over decades—perhaps centuries—and was now a withered brown.

But any shortcomings simply added to the romantic charm. Who might have slept here—made love here 200 years ago? What were they like? What mystery and adventure just being here! If we squinted just a bit, it all looked brand new. If I closed my eyes ,I could feel the original occupants—almost smell their perfume; powdered wigs, beauty marks, impossible gravity-defying coiffure. We spent a moment clinging to each other.

We dressed for dinner and found the young man who had since put on a jacket and had become the Directeur de l'hôtel. He escorted us to the formal library and excused himself for a moment. The room was cold. Hanging on the walls were several life-size paintings of folks who must have been the original royal residents.

The walls were covered in beautiful frescos of the surrounding landscape. The crown moldings were covered with a veneer of gilt. Ornate corbels jutted from where the walls met ceiling. They supported the weight of the centuries.

The young man appeared again, this time as a simple 'serveur'—a waiter—with bow tie and a small tray balancing two glasses of aperitif. He took our dinner order, *poulet* or *boeuf*. And as he left, he stopped at a very old phonograph, placed the needle on an old 78 rpm record and retired. A scratchy Edith Piaf sang "La Vie en Rose," *"Et dès que je l'aperçois, Alors je sens en moi Mon cœur qui bat."* ("and from the things that I sense, I feel within me a heart that beats")

We sipped and reveled and were glad we were alive and so grateful to our daughter.

The ubiquitous little man returned again, this time in an apron with a hand towel draped across his arm. He escorted us to our table in the dining room. We were the only guests. It was late when we finished. We thanked our host and retreated to our room, exhausted. We retired in each other's arms.

France was a whirlwind four days of rushing to see all we could before leaving for an exciting six-day adventure with Tara in Italy.

We took the train from Paris to Rome, enjoying the gregarious Italians who joined us and catching a wink or two en route. But we were mostly awake and excited about visiting Rome. We weren't disappointed.

Our budget plunked us in a funky four-story walk up next to the bustling Campo di Fiori alive with vendors, flowers, fruits, vegetables and a plethora of palate-pleasing treats.

We loved Rome. We saw all we could in the two days we had before tooting off for Florence; St. Peter's and the Pieta, Coliseum, the Forum, Arch of Constantine, Palatine Hill, Circus Maximus, Pantheon, all the fountains and the food. We went to the Vatican and waved back at the Pope and yelled "yoo hoo" which, I'm told, is Latin for "Hello up there Mr. Pope." And we ate gelato and more gelato and more gelato. We promised ourselves we would come back. We said, "Arivederci Roma," and looked forward to Florence—Firenze.

An Early Departure

Firenze was more spectacular than we expected. One could spend a week in the Uffizi Museum and still not see it all. But we got there late in the afternoon and had to run through the imposingly long corridors lined with extraordinary sculptures, bouncing from gallery to gallery trying to see it all in three hours.

We flew from the flat, two dimensional art of the 14th century to the Gothic period, through the early Renaissance of Masaccio and Uccello running past Tiziano, Lippi and Botticelli to catch glimpses of Michelangelo, Rembrandt, Caravaggio and Da Vinci. Room after room of absolutely amazing—totally engrossing miraculous God-given human talent.

Wow! What fun!

I was proud to be Italian. I thought it might be nice to live here—somewhere in the Tuscan hills where the lemons are as big as oranges and the oranges as big as grapefruits. And I would eat real Italian pizza every day and—and gelato—ahhh the gelato.

We saw the seventeen-foot statue of the David by Michelangelo, visited the market, the Ponte Vecchio, and shopped for leather and gold. We were sad to leave, knowing our last stop, Venice, was the end of our adventure. We couldn't know that the most memorable event in our journey was about to occur.

We got to the Florence train station very early the day of our departure. I didn't want to take any chances on getting lost or not having done something. We checked in and took the escalator up to the terminal. I checked the big "Arrivals/Departures" board to be sure I had the correct time and track. Yes, there it was: **Firenze a Venezia** departing 9:00, track number 11.

It was only 7:15. We had plenty of time. The train was just sitting there. I got on, and Les and Tara passed the luggage up to me. I staked out a perfect cozy compartment for the four of us. Tara volunteered to go and check on our reservation from Venice back to Rome, so Les and I waited on the platform. A minute or two later three chubby elderly women came chugging along huffing and puffing with their luggage in hand. "Ladies, Signore, lenta, lenta, you can slow down, the train doesn't leave for some time yet." I mounted the train and helped them on board with their luggage.

"Oh, my, my, my!" (They were apparently Americans.) She continued, "We were so worried we would miss the train." I stepped back down from the train smiled with sincere compassion and said, "Don't worry, the train doesn't leave for more than an hour." One of the old ladies looked surprised and said, "Really, the man over on track 3 told us we had to hurry over to track 11 if we wanted to catch the 7:30 train to Rome."

"To Rome!" I thought. "Someone has seriously misled these poor old ladies."

"I'm awfully sorry to tell you ladies, but this train is going to Venice. See—up there on the board: Venice, track 11 at 9:00."

"Oh, my what will we do now?" I asked if I could help them with their luggage. "No thanks, we'll manage." and they shuffled off to find their train to Rome.

Les got on the train, and I watched for Tara. I looked at my watch, then at the big clock above the 'big board'—7:30. I started to turn to say something to Les, but before I uttered a word the steps to the train disappeared, the doors slammed closed and the train began to move. It didn't happen slowly. There was no warning—no "ALL ABOARD!" Things didn't happen in a progression. It happened all at once. The train was on its way in a split second—the blink of an eye—the snap of fingers.

And-it **was** the 7:30 train to Rome!

I started yelling "Oh, my God! Stopa the train! Stopa the traino" "Basta, Arresto. STOPA." But the train quickly picked up speed. I continued to holler "Stopa the train! Stopa the train!" People just looked at me. I ran after it but realized,

It'll Be Okay In The Morning

"What will I do if I catch it?" There was nothing to hang on to—no way to get on.

Les was gone, along with all the luggage but no passport, no money and unable to speak a word of Italian. She was gone! Just like that. Maybe forever. I had to get her back! Then! "Oh my God, What do I tell my beautiful, wonderful, trusting daughter?" That would have to wait.

I ran to the police office in the terminal. I made them understand that "Mi wife *venti* a Roma on the wronga *trano*! Un grande errore—big mistake!" I kept repeating the message stumbling between bad Italian and bad English until they got the point. "*Ah, Senor non fa niente.*" (Don't worry about it) "*Otterremo tua moglie indietro per voi.*" (We will get your wife back for you.) "*I treno si ferma ad Arezzo.*" (The train will stop at, Arezzo.) "*Sara presto.*" (She will be back soon.) Somewhat relieved, I ran and caught Tara as she emerged from Tickets/Reservations. "Oh, Hi Dad. We're all set for the trip back. I got us a compartment. Where's Mom?"

I hadn't thought through what I was going to say. "Ah, uhm, ahh, Mom—Oh yes—Mom. Well ya see, actually—Mom got on the wrong train and—she's ah, on her way to Rome—BUT don't worry; we'll get her back soon."

Forty minutes later as I was waiting, thumbing through an Italian version of Playboy, Les' voice came booming, ricocheting off the ceramic walls of the huge Florence terminal, "Briaaaaan! <u>WHAT</u> are you doing! Is this the best you can do? Don't you realize I could have died, and all you can do is look at *girlie* magazines? If I had to leave it up to you, I'd still be on my way to Rome. It's a good thing I made them stop the train. I made some little man help me across the tracks with all our luggage."

I thought, "She doesn't realize I had the train stopped in Arezzo. No sense in arguing. She's had a scary, bad morning. I felt a sorry for the little man, whoever he was.

We had a nice time in Venice—brief but nice. St. Mark's Square was remarkable, and the canals and the food fabulous, but Venice seemed to us a little spoiled—a little too commercial. Maybe we were just too tired—too rushed.

We said our good byes and boarded the overnight train back to Paris for our flight home. We dozed, and as the sun rose, we opened our eyes to see the snow-covered Alps lining the train route. majestic, imposing, cold and brilliant, they stood at attention and saluted a farewell as we passed.

It was a magic trip—memories to last a lifetime, but we promised ourselves we would come back to Italy. We did! And there have been so many other exciting adventures for us.

Les and I have seen so much of the world: hiked high above the sky-blue Mediterranean on the Walk of the Gods between Amalfi and Positano, ridden horses through the forests of the Apennine Mountains, hiked in the Dolomites.

We visited the untouristy city and cathedral of Loreto in which the home of the Virgin Mary was reconstructed hundreds of years ago and in which countless miraculous cures have occurred. Miracles still happen there like little bolts of lightening. The cathedral square teemed with the wheel chairs and litters of the sick and infirm, all praying for their own little bolt from heaven. We stopped by the little town of Cocullo just after their annual Feast of the Serpents in which they honor their patron Saint Domenico by draping his statue with hundreds of live snakes, and we listened to a classical guitar concert in Ravello.

We have visited friends in Austria, seen Mozart's home in Salzburg, toured Lake Wolfgang and taken the cog railway to the top of the world high above the clouds.

We walked the quiet, empty beaches of the Caribbean's faraway places with strange sounding names, Bequia, Mustique, Cooper Union, Saba, Tortola, Virgin Gorda. We enjoyed pristine Hawaii long before it became endless beaches of high-rise hotels, and we bathed, hidden from the world, in the secret hot springs of King Kamehameha.

We visited Egypt and stayed with good friends. We experienced Cairo unlike other tourists, escorted by Egyptian aristocracy. They gave us a unique view of their treasures; the pyramids, the City of the Dead, the Khan el-Khalili market where we haggled for some gold for Les, the National Museum—King Tut and mummies. We walked along the Nile in Cairo at night unescorted, toured Abu Cymbal, the Valley of the Kings and Sharm el-Sheik.

We've gone on African safari and have been close enough to lions to hear them purr and smell their breath.

We've visited Ireland and met my remaining Irish relatives who live on the beautiful lough my mother so often spoke of.

We have climbed together to the top of the Canadian Rockies and looked down on Lake Louise. And we've seen the very best of this great land. I've climbed up our own Rockies and descended down, down, down to the bottom of the Grand Canyon.

And through all this I have only nearly lost Les on one or two other occasions—when she forgot to get off ski lifts here and there, continuing on up the mountains; her head held high facing the unknown. But she always found a way back. We've never had another episode to equal her side trip to Arezzo.

Chapter 49.
Capitulation

After almost going totally blind, Chris went back to Kent, but there were no new friends. The chip on his shoulder grew bigger, and one day he "cold cocked" his roommate with a hockey stick, unable to take the persistent harangue any longer.

He stopped doing any more work at Kent. He just refused—just sat! We had no choice but to pull him out and send him to New Milford High School. We might just as well have flushed him down a toilet. But there was no place else.

National Geographic Episode: A mother caribou tries to protect her newborn from a pack of ravenous wolves. One wolf attacks from the left. The mother turns, only to have another nip at the calf from the right. On and on the wolves attack and torment until the mother is too exhausted to carry on and the calf succumbs to the attacks. The mother, no longer physically capable of intervening, only watches as her child is torn apart.

I sometimes felt like that, watching my son psychologically, emotionally torn apart by the demons that tormented him. Les and I wore down. We blamed ourselves and each other.

Shortly after Chris began at New Milford High, he finally made friends and began to numb his pain. But the friends were just a bunch of pot-smoking losers. It was the pot and the 'mushrooms' and LSD that were the friends. We watched it happen. Like watching a man drown, unable to reach him. I didn't want to believe it. I insisted it was something else.

I waited up for him the first night he came home drunk. He staggered in, and I watched, hoping he was just tired or had momentarily lost his balance. But I couldn't ignore it. "Chris, you're drunk!" He slurred back, "I'm sorry Dad."

We made him help at the local soup kitchen for several hours, hoping he might "get it." He didn't.

We went away for a weekend to visit friends in New Jersey, leaving Chris at home by himself. He was fifteen, and we were sure he could manage. Chris secretly decided to have a party. As soon as we returned home, we knew something was wrong. The house smelled. The basement floor was sticky. We looked more closely: some walls were stained, some things were missing. We confronted Chris and were met with initial denial. We interrogated him further and found that he had invited a few friends over. But word spread among his new "pot head" friends, and scores of kids showed up, some forcing their way in. In a panic Chris called on a good friend and neighbor, John Wakely. John heroically came to Chris' aide and turned back the invaders. John never told us. Maybe he wanted to save us the embarrassment; maybe he wanted to save Chris the shame. Chris tried to put the house back together with a little help from others, but it was like trying to clean the decks of an aircraft carrier with a toothbrush.

Summer! We hoped for a reprieve—a fresh start, but Les began finding evidence—pot-smoking paraphernalia. At first I blocked the information pretending it was something else. I didn't want to believe it because I didn't know what to do about it. So, insanely, I kept driving Chris to "friend's" homes and congregating places, convincing myself they were okay, not wanting him to be totally alone. Rationalizing, *I can't just let him sit alone at home with no friends.* I thought it was compassion at the time.

Chris then began to hang around John O'Hara.

Chapter 50.
John O'Hara

John O'Hara was a boisterous, beer-drinking Irishman who taught high school general science in Long Island. He spent summers and weekends in his house in our little Deer Run Shores community for close to 15 years—long before we got there. He was an original Deer Run Shores pioneer.

John was a bachelor and lived with another bachelor teacher. He was loud and obnoxious with a gravel voice. When John went down to the Deer Run Shores docks, you could hear that gravel voice bouncing off all the surrounding hills like finger nails scratching against the blackboard sky and ripping up the pine trees.

Other than being loud and uncouth, John was considered okay. He spent a lot of time in the summer sharing his 300-horsepower ski boat with friends, many of whom were Deer Run Shores pre-teen and teenage boys. They all loved water skiing and just cruising around the lake gawking at pretty girls in skimpy bathing suits. Parents didn't entirely approve of John, but in our small town water skiing was a welcome diversion for the kids in the summer, and most gave their approval although with undisguised "harrumphs."

In the summer of his sixteenth year, after flunking every subject and repeatedly being caught and penalized for drug use, Chris and his good friend John were among O'Hara's followers. There was little else for Chris to do. I didn't like John O'Hara, but he had apparently been a mentor and friend to many boys over the years. My "harrumph" notwithstanding, John and his boat became a welcome diversion. I hoped he might be a positive influence.

The summer days passed. When I was home on weekends, we went out in our own ski boat, swam in the lake and Chris tooled around on his ATV. And he filled in time with his friend John and John O'Hara.

One evening when it was getting late and Chris had not come home, I asked where he was. Les wasn't sure. I called John's mother. She said she thought Chris and John had gone to O'Hara's. I called O'Hara and asked to speak to Chris. His gravel voice was strained, "Oh, ah, yeah, Chris. Just a minute." There was awkward silence, muffled comments. Something was very wrong. My mind raced. Dark thoughts. I put the phone down, rushed to my car and catapulted to O'Hara's house. I didn't knock, just pushed through the front door of the raised ranch. John's roommate was calmly watching TV. I asked where John was and he motioned downstairs.

I raced down the stairs! The gravel voice, "Hey Mr. C how you doin'? Chris was just about to leave."
I said nothing except, "Chris and John, let's go."

I never asked Chris all of what had happened. I didn't report O'Hara to the police.

Chris told me that O'Hara gave him and the other boys Vodka, but that's all he volunteered.

I was angry at what O'Hara had tried to do. How could I make a statement, pay him back, get even, if only a little? I could never really get even. I had to do something.

It'll Be Okay In The Morning

Summer ended, and by lottery some lucky few residents were allowed to store their boats in our clubhouse. John O'Hara was one of those lucky ones. I promised myself I had to do something for revenge, even if I knew it was stupid—trivial.

One winter night I skulked down to the deserted clubhouse. The sliding glass doors were locked, but somehow I found strength enough to lift the entire 4-by-8-foot glass door out of its track and access the boats. I stood in front of O'Hara's boat and asked myself, "So, what the hell are you doing here? What are you going to do now, idiot?" I had no tools, but I was able to remove all the hardware from the steering gear that controlled the I/O motor so that the boat would be unusable come spring. I replaced the door and hurled the parts into the lake. Not much of a statement, but I couldn't kill him.

Spring came, and John had his boat repaired, and every time I heard that gravel voice coming from the docks below I couldn't think of anything but more revenge.

Another silly, sick, idea hatched.

For the next month I collected my own personal urine in an empty gallon bleach bottle. I filled it to the brim. Then on a dark, rainy night when there was no one at the docks and no one boating the next day, I sneaked down to the lake. With the rain pouring down in the black night, I located O'Hara's boat. I lifted the canvas and poured the gallon of urine on its floor to sit and spread and soak stink. I felt better.

I never saw or heard of any reaction from O'Hara to the putrid ammonia stench that must have wafted up when he next lifted the cover of that boat. I like to believe I smelled it all the way up on my deck a quarter mile away.

Chapter 51.
A Decisive Year— Intervention

The summer ended, and a new school year began with trepidation—and for good reason. Soon the high school was sending us notifications that Chris was skipping classes. We had meetings with the principal and teachers. But he went on to fail every subject in that semester. We responded by threatening and grounding him. It didn't do any good. Everyone threw up their hands. He just sat!

We began recording phone conversations between him and his drug-using friends to reconfirm what we knew but didn't want to believe. I listened to the conversations. Was this really my son? "Hey Dude, got any f——- sh—? Wanna get f——- up tonight? I'll get a ride. No, they don't know sh—. Yeah man, we'll get f——- up good."

This **is** my son!

Our family was falling apart. I began losing my temper.

Our neighbor, Jim Law, offered Chris a job, paying him well to mow his lawn. But Chris couldn't get out of bed—couldn't remember to do it. Jim Law's grass grew. And I watched and I counseled and implored, yelled and screamed. But I couldn't get Chris to change, and when he looked at me with a "fuck you, you can't make me" smirk I knocked him down the garage stairs and on another occasion grabbed him by the throat.

Chris continued to drown. We ran here and there along the sidelines looking for help, watching him go under.

We finally found help. My employer's insurance enabled us to send Chris to Hazelton/St. Mary's in Minneapolis, the best inpatient rehabilitation facility in the country. One catch: Chris had to agree to go.

With the help of a local support group we planned an intervention. The process required people who loved Chris to confront him—people he might trust. They would hold up a mirror so Chris could see what he had become.

My sister Sheila and her husband Michael joined us in the intervention; both had their lives sidetracked by alcoholism and were long-time veterans of AA. Les' Mom and Dad were also there. We contrived a strategy to get him to the intervention without his suspecting. I prayed, "God, please do not let him find out—don't let him suspect." I was sure if he did, he would run away, maybe never to be seen again. Maybe one day his bones would be found in a Brazilian jungle. The natives would tell us he died after chewing peyote for years, finally ending his life trying to fly off a cliff to join the monkey god.

But we pulled it off. Chris stepped into the room. I expected him to run away, but he frowned and listened to the counselor's well-rehearsed explanation of what was about to take place. "Chris, all these people have gathered here today to tell you that they love you and are extremely worried about you. They want you to hear them out. If you have a response, you can offer it at the end."

One by one the participants lambasted Chris with their sincere love and fear for his future—fear for his life. I was saved for last. I had to deliver the ultimatum. "Chris you've

It'll Be Okay In The Morning

heard all these people who love you. We all are extremely worried about you. Your Mom and I have been frightened and crying for more than a year knowing you were on drugs while you denied it. But we hired a detective (I lied) and know the people you buy from. We know you have stolen from us ,and we know the people you use with. We don't want to see you dead. We want to help you save yourself." I held my breath as I said, "So you have a choice to make today—right now. We've made arrangements for you to go to Minneapolis to the best treatment facility we could find. I'll take you, and we leave tonight. If you choose not to go, we don't want you back home. You'll have to find someplace else to live."

He responded. "Why do I have to go away? I can do it here? It's not that bad. I can stop any time." Finally, "Screw it! I'm not going." And he walked out into the cold, late afternoon.

The semi-circle of loved ones was speechless. They raised eyebrows and wrung their hands in worry for our nearly dearly departed. I consulted with Michael and Sheila, who had a lifetime of experience between them. "Narc Angel" Michael and I ran after Chris and tracked him down a few blocks away. It was bitterly cold. Chris was bitterly furious. I was bitterly frightened. He argued, but Michael convinced him there really was no alternative.

We had already packed bags and were ready to go. I was afraid he would change his mind before we got to Minneapolis. And he did several times. He hated me. I didn't trust him.

Michael drove us to LaGuardia. I was exhausted, running on empty, numb during the hour-and-a-half ride.

The flight was uneventful. There was no conversation. By the time we got to Minneapolis at about 10:00 that night, I was exhausted. We checked into the Radisson hotel. I kept watching Chris, waiting for him to bolt or do something stupid.

We checked into our room. It was midnight in Connecticut. I felt like I had been on a three-day bivouac—no sleep and no chance to wash. My skin was tacky. The day's nervous sweat had built up in layers and dried like a pair of thin, smelly long underwear. I could have peeled it off. I needed a shower, but I was afraid to leave Chris alone even for moment. I chanced it, turning on the shower and peeking out of the bathroom door several times to see what he might do in my absence. I jumped in and out checking and rechecking to be sure; of what, I didn't know. I ran the little domino-sized bar of soap across my body once or twice and considered myself clean. I felt better.

We went to bed shortly after, and I lay there with one eye open, feeling sorry for myself. I must have fallen asleep for a short time, but my eyes were open as the night dissolved into a sad, gray bitter Minnesota morning.

I woke Chris without conversation. We ate in a mélange of steely silence: fear and hope and anger and lopsided love.

The cab ride to St. Mary's was mercifully brief, each of us looking out our separate windows, struggling to say nothing. The greeting and the check-in at St. Mary's were uneventful. They asked me to wait while they inspected Chris' luggage to be sure he had everything he needed and nothing more. We filled the cracks with useless blather in the brief time left to us. The "keepers" returned too soon. "Chris, you can come with me now." We rose together. The

It'll Be Okay In The Morning

hugs and the "I love you's" were exchanged with stubbornly withheld emotion.

The remaining counselor and I watched him walk off.

The counselor turned to me, "Mr. Cosacchi, you may not have missed this yet but we doubt you gave it to Chris." He handed me a fifty-dollar bill Chris had somehow stolen from my wallet during the night. *Yes, it's mine*, I thought. How in God's name could Chris have gotten hold of it? I had taken every precaution, jumping in and out of the shower, never letting him out of my sight, sleeping on my clothes and wallet. I was amazed at the ingenious dexterity of the drug addict. But on reflection I shouldn't have been so surprised. I remembered the money he had stolen from piggy banks and purses and Les' treasured collection of rare silver dollars he had pawned.

I left with the fifty dollars, shaking my head. I cried a little in the cab to the airport. I cried a lot later.

We visited Chris while he was in rehab, Les once by herself, and once together. Christopher did not return home for six months.

While Chris was gone, we fought for some help for his education from the State. We wanted to send him to a special school, and we asked for an amount equal to whatever the state would have to spend to send him to New Milford High. They finally gave in, and Chris was able to spend his last year of high school at the prestigious Foreman School in Litchfield, a school for kids with learning disabilities.

Our hopes grew as he made some good friends, passed his courses and did well enough in his SAT's to be accepted at a few colleges. We had no way of knowing that the college we chose, the beautiful, pristine College of Charleston in Charleston, South Carolina, would be another mistake.

Chapter 52.
Good Bye John

While Chris attended the Foreman School, the three of us occasionally went out for dinner at Alfredo's, our local "checkered table cloth" Italian restaurant. One evening as we seated ourselves, we froze and looked at each other. That voice! We recognized that voice—that laugh—gurgly, gravel, growing, rising rudely above other conversation. O'Hara!

Chris was calm on the outside. We all were. "I wish I could confront him," Chris whispered. I whispered back, "Why don't you?" Chris sat quietly for a moment then purposefully rose, turned and walked back toward the voice. We couldn't hear much of the conversation. "Hey, Chris!" John O'Hara yelled. He extended his hand. Chris didn't take it.

There were three other people at the table. We only heard snippets of Chris' monologue: "So John,...friends...vodka...kids?" Then silence. No more gurgly gravel voice. Chris returned to the table. I was proud of him.

We ate. All of our appetites were satisfied.

A month later we read in the morning paper, on page two: "Deer Run Shores Resident Takes His Life." John O'Hara had blown his head off with a shotgun. Maybe he would have done it even if Chris hadn't "outed" him in front of his friends. Then again, maybe he wouldn't have. Either way, good riddance.

Chapter 53.
Charleston—Meet Lisa

In the fall of 1990, after graduating The Foreman School, Chris was off to The College of Charleston. We were optimistic once again that he would find his way.

But he flunked out in his first semester and remained in Charleston working, selling ice cream from a pushcart on the Charleston streets. It was sometime during this year or so that he met Lisa Pierotti.

I don't recall when we first met her—sometime in 1996. We were in the process of moving to Hilton Head to retire early and escape New England winters. She was Chris' new girlfriend, tall, fairly attractive with long light brown hair down to her waist. But, to me, Lisa had an over-the-top, know it all, "I'm great aren't I!" attitude that offset her good looks. We didn't know very much about her other than her last name was Pierotti, and she was from Los Alamos, New Mexico.

My first impression of Lisa was that she was a bullshitter. But I didn't anticipate the harm she would cause. She is seriously mentally ill. Her drug and alcohol addiction and the fact that she has never admitted her illnesses to herself tragically compound her illness.

On a trip from Charleston to Hilton Head not long after our meeting, Lisa asked me bluntly, "So, what are your first impressions?" I responded bluntly, "I think you're a bullshitter." I didn't tell her how much I disliked her, but I know it must have shown, leaking out my nose, my ears.

But Lisa had a hard life. She told us she saw her father abuse her mother. She was kicked out of her home when she was just 17. Her father told her to break off with her motorcycle boyfriend, but she refused. He declared the ultimatum, "our way or the highway." Lisa chose the highway.

She has been home only on rare occasions over the past 20 years, and then only for very short periods. She has had to live without help, without family, alone with her illness. Her parents say they love her, but there is no doubt that they don't miss her; no doubt that they are glad—relieved—that she is two thousand miles away. Her parents regret maybe having brought her into this world at all.

Chapter 54.
A Difficult Retirement

We settled into our comfortable early retirement. We didn't see much of Chris and Lisa during the first couple of years, even though they were only two hours away. Then, in 1998, they began the precipitous downward slide that lasted more than a decade.

They were arrested for possession of marijuana with intent to distribute. They had hooked up with another pair of idiots who were importing marijuana through the mail from California. The postal authorities discovered a shipment, and the police raided the apartment where the group was breaking it down. All four were arrested. Chris and Lisa pled out the charges—"No Contest." Each ended up with a felony conviction, though they didn't have to serve any time. The other two partners had strong local Charleston connections and got off with just a slap on the wrist.

After their conviction we hoped the worst was over. They moved to Hilton Head, and we bought them a town home. They paid us reasonable rent, and we promised if they did well, a portion of the rent would be applied to principle—just like a mortgage with no down payment. But after less than a year they relapsed, and they lost all of what little they had.

They left Hilton Head Island with nothing. We were glad to see them go. We didn't care where they went as long as they were out of our life.

They were street-smart survivors and knew how to milk the system. So with no place else to go, rehab was the best, if not the only alternative to the gutter. Chris completed his third rehab. Lisa was kicked out. She has been kicked out of all eight or ten treatment facilities she has entered over the years for a variety of offenses: cheating, stealing, lying and an aggressive, threatening in-your-face attitude.

After rehab they reconnected and settled, this time, in Rock Hill, South Carolina. Chris went back to school. Lisa found work at a Winn Dixie supermarket and began to receive psychiatric help at Catawba Mental Health in Rock Hill. We were guardedly optimistic that and things would get better.

We naively thought they were doing okay. We believed what we wanted to, sticking our heads in the sand. We prayed that Lisa would not get pregnant.

No prayer goes unanswered, and in October of 1999 Chris called to tell us, "Lisa's pregnant."

God said, "No."

There was nothing we could do. And we felt sooner or later we would have to help with whatever mess they created.

I began a new game of *what if-ing*, playing with possibilities, like a game of Cats in the Cradle, pulling apart and reshaping the threads of our life with theirs. I thought pessimistically about how they screwed up our life. I imagined horrible things so that when *it* happened, *it* wouldn't be a shock, and anything short of my pessimistic supposings would make *it* easier to bear.

It'll Be Okay In The Morning

In May of 2000 they brought Christopher Michael Cosacchi into this world, a handsome, charming little baby boy. We prayed for a miracle that would make his life okay.

Chapter 55.
A Christmas To Remember

Months passed. We extended an olive branch and invited them all down for Christopher's first Christmas.

When they arrived, I swore I smelled brimstone. Something was wrong with Lisa. She couldn't shut up, couldn't focus on anything. She talked non-stop. "Oh, I'm so glad it's Christmas. I just love Christmas. Don't you love it? Look at the beautiful tree. O*hit'ssuchabeautifultree.IjustloveChristmasdon't*you? I do. It's so lovely the tree and all. You know, the decorations and the carols and the tree. Oh, the tree is so beautiful. Don't you think it's beautiful? I think it's beautiful…"

When she carried Christopher, she swung him around like a loaf of bread. We instinctively reached out and gasped as his head missed door jams and walls by an inch or two. She became irate because there was no 5:00 o'clock mass on Christmas Eve at St. Francis By the Sea Catholic Church. She wanted to take little Christopher. No matter that she couldn't tell you the last time she was in a church.

There was that smell of brimstone again.

She called the church. "What do you mean you will not be having a 5:00 o'clock mass on Christmas Eve! Well, that's ridiculous! Who ever heard of such a thing? Where do you people get off anyway? That's terrible. Are you sure you are a ROMAN Catholic Church? That's ridiculous. All real Catholic churches have 5:00 o'clock mass on Christmas Eve. I should report you. You're ridiculous!"

And so it continued into the night. We were frightened and held our breath wondering, worrying what she might do.

At about 9:00 pm she told us she still had to wrap a few presents. We supplied her with all the materials and tools she needed, and she retired to the little windowless sewing room. At 10:00 Les went to bed, and shortly thereafter Chris retired. I decided to stay up and see how Lisa was doing. At about 11:00 I checked in on her. She was sitting on the floor in a corner of the little room with paper strewn about amid a variety of miscellaneous gift-wrapping paraphernalia. There were no wrapped packages. She had a vacant look and began to cry. I tried to console her and get her to retire, but she insisted on continuing. I stayed up until she went to bed at about 1:00 in the morning, worried about what might happen to her, worried about what she might do accidentally or otherwise.

I tried to be encouraging—sympathetic. I didn't sleep much remembering other nights as a kid when the world was upside down and screams and shouts from downstairs kept us awake. I remembered telling myself so long ago, *If I can just stay awake everything will be okay in the morning.* It wasn't then. It wasn't now.

The morning arrived, and we began where we left off. Les and I walked on eggshells looking out of the corners of our eyes at each other, waiting, watching. Lisa came to breakfast wearing a provocative, diaphanous, somewhat revealing garment. She looked cheap. I was embarrassed for her and found myself looking at the walls and the stairs and carpet and my shoes.

She became distracted by everything around her and couldn't keep track of Christopher as he wandered off here and there. Les and I had to be sure one of us was attentive to his whereabouts. Tension grew through breakfast, like a crescendo looking for a drum roll and a cymbal crash.

We started to open gifts. Lisa began taking photographs of everyone and everything trying to hold on to the moment—to capture it inside the camera. Nothing could escape, or the whole thing would be ruined. Click, click, snap, snap, close-ups, photos and telephotos, flash and no flash, twenty, thirty, forty, fifty, one hundred photos. Her excitement was uncontrolled. She snapped away; pictures of the baby, and the baby with his toys, and the gifts, the towels and the clock and the dishes and photos of cat and the tree and the carpet and the pine needles and the gift wrap and bows and boxes and us and her and breakfast and the coffee pot, the leftovers and the kitchen sink.

We gently said, "Gee, Lisa, why don't we take a break from the photos for a moment," only to be met with a Redstone rocket-sized tirade of irate indignation. As the morning torturously continued, the atmosphere plummeted. Lisa lurched into a tornado of nonstop philosophy on Christmas, lectures on what it should be and how much it meant to her. She had the floor and was on a frenzied, flipped out filibuster. Finally, as she careened toward an emotional cliff, in desperation we called the Catawba Mental Health Clinic. The on-duty counselor urged us to get her to an emergency room right away.

By this time Lisa was alternating from crying to laughing to lecturing, again swinging the baby around like a loaf of bread. At that moment she must have realized she was in trouble. She offered no argument.

The emergency room was quiet. There were no signs of Christmas. The attending physician saw Lisa in private. When he returned, he told us he had administered enough Ativan intravenously to knock out a horse, and still Lisa did not "come down." He gave us additional Ativan pills to help her normalize.

We returned home. Lisa quieted. It was getting late. Les and I went to bed staring at each other.
"God help that little boy."
"What's going to happen to him—to all of them?"
"Maybe Chris will get better one day. Maybe he'll be able to be a good father." And we turned away to sleep.

They returned to Rock Hill the next morning, and we fretted and worried. It was their life, their son, and their problems.

Chapter 56.
The Inevitable

A few months passed before the next emergency call. Lisa had called the police, accusing Chris of domestic violence. He told us he was just trying to get away—trying to get on his bike—when Lisa tried to grab his cell phone from his pocket. But Lisa's neighbor told the police she saw the episode, and Chris was arrested. He was released but didn't return home.

The following day Lisa called and begged us to come and get the baby because she couldn't manage alone. For just a second I asked myself, "Should I go? Should we get involved?" Then I jumped into the car and began to drive fast enough to acknowledge the crisis but slow enough to continue asking myself, "Am I doing the right thing?" I called Lisa while en route to let her know my estimated arrival time. She was agitated and launched into a tirade, screaming at me at the top of her lungs. I heard Christopher crying in the background and tried to tell Lisa to stop screaming for the baby's sake, but she couldn't hear me over her own screaming, and I found myself screaming back, "Lisa, stop—stop screaming—the baby—the baby!"

When I arrived, she and her neighbor were trying to get little Christopher ready. The apartment looked a shambles as if a free-for-all had taken place; clothes and dirty dishes strewn about. A framed photo of Les and me teetered sideways on the wall. We looked out from the photo through smashed glass. I thought, "Why are we smiling?" Little Christopher was a mess, dressed in just a diaper and a

T-shirt covered in sticky, red Kool-Aid. Lisa was stuffing clean clothes and dirty clothes together into a garbage bag that was to be his suitcase. Christopher looked confused and befuddled as Mom rushed him out the door.

I drove home with him in his back seat booster chair. I sang some silly songs and let him sleep. Adjusting the rear view mirror downward I could see him; a little, chunky, slumped-over package drifting, resting. Over the next few years and maybe a hundred trips I watched that little package grow in his booster seat, never complaining, never crying. That little boy would melt your heart.

We returned Christopher after a few days when things seemed to settle down and Chris had returned home. When we arrived, we thought we were prepared, but Lisa was out of control again, lashing out. Even with Chris there it made us fear for the baby. I was afraid to stay. Les was afraid to leave. I left. She stayed.

When I returned to pick up Les, Chris had decided to leave Lisa and take Christopher with him.

When Lisa left for work that morning, I returned, and the four of us fled to a motel to hide until we could decide what to do.

We found an attorney for Chris in Rock Hill and went to court to help Chris get his first legal separation and custody of his son. I testified. Chris' AA sponsor showed up to support him. Joe was in his seventies. He had been sober for more than thirty years, and he believed in Chris. I think he loved him like a son and though AA sponsors are warned not to get emotionally tied to their sponsees, Joe sat next to me and cried. He had been through so much in his own life it hurt him deeply to watch Chris and this family dissolve.

We were thankful that an end had come to this travesty of a marriage; relieved little Christopher wouldn't have to live his life dealing with his mother's insanity and the constant worry of repeated violence. We knew we would have to help, but it would be worth our peace of mind.

But it wasn't to be. Chris and Lisa didn't really break up. While they had separate apartments a few miles apart, Lisa was a welcome and almost permanent guest in Chris' home. We didn't know. We felt great compassion for Chris, wondering how a legally blind Dad could take care of his son alone. We helped a little financially each month and brought Christopher down to Hilton Head every other weekend to give his Dad what we thought was a needed break.

We found out we had been 'played' and that they were still together when Chris called and told us Lisa had attacked him and he had called the police. The police came but ignored the scratches and cuts on his face and blamed him. No arrests were made. No charges were filed. And so it started all over.

Chapter 57.
—And then there were Two

In 2003 Chris received his bachelor's degree in social work from Winthrop University but couldn't find a job because of his felony conviction five years earlier. Lisa was fired from her job at Winn Dixie Supermarket for insubordination. She found another job as a waitress. They both started using marijuana again, and before long they turned to cocaine.

The phone rang one morning in June. Les answered. It was Chris. I knew it was bad news. It almost always was.

I caught just a word or two of Les' conversation, "You're kidding. When?"

I didn't need to hear any more. I just knew from all my supposings and began shouting out loud as if the yelling would keep the news from getting through, "Oh no, please, God. OH NO! La la la la I can't hear you!"

Lisa was pregnant again.

Chris told Les that they both thought having another child would help their marriage. We just shook our heads.

Briana Faith Cosacchi was born on March 29, 2004, a tiny thing. She came with a cleft pallet—probably a result of Lisa's taking drugs while she was pregnant. Her birth fixed nothing.

Violence continued to pepper the marriage.

One cold day in 2005 a fight broke out in their little house. Lisa fled into the gray winter day half dressed. Chris ran after her, struggling, grabbing her by the hair, yanking, pulling, trying to get her back inside. A neighbor watched the scene and called the police. Chris was arrested again.

Rather than go to jury trial he pled "no contest" at the recommendation of his Public Defender.

Several months passed, and by November 2005 drugs had again taken over. And now there were two children.

About a week before Thanksgiving of 2005 Lisa called, crying, hysterical. "You have to come and get the children. Please! Please! Chris and I have been using drugs, and we haven't been able to stop. Chris is out on the street now looking for more. He doesn't know I'm calling. But I'm afraid for the kids. Please come and take them."

Her confession left no doubt. She wasn't kidding, and the kids were in danger. We jumped in the car and raced the 120 miles to exit 159 off Interstate 26—a halfway point between Hilton Head and Rock Hill. Lisa arrived shortly after. The car flew into the parking lot. A moment's pause, then Lisa leaped from the car, her waist-long tresses trailing behind her like a jet stream. She looked gaunt—pasty from lack of sleep and days of drug use. She hustled the startled children to our car along with a disorganized array of luggage; garbage bags, little suitcases with pieces of clothing, jammed, stuck, peeking from the corners.

"Thank you. Oh God, thank you so much for coming. I don't know what I would have done." She was near panic, going off like a firecracker salute. "We have to stop the drugs. We will! I know we will! It's been a big mistake. We're going to stop. But we need a little time. We can't have the kids right now."

I embarked on a pretentious lecture. "Lisa, you can't do this alone. You need help, and if you don't get help—if you don't stop the drugs, we will have to get DSS (Department of Social Services) involved and they might take the children."

"I know, I know, we have to get help. We will. I promise. We will. Thank you. Thank you. I know you'll take good care of the kids."

I repeated the warning. I needed to be sure she understood that we would call Social Services if they didn't get help. She repeated her understanding, and we parted. I let out a sigh. The drive home was quiet, though I sang some silly songs again. We tried to be reassuring. It was hard.

Two old people with two babies maybe forever—probably forever. We needed reassurance too. I thought, "Maybe all those other tragedies were God's way of toughening us up for this."

Chris called the following day asking for the children back, blaming Lisa, telling us she started back on drugs first by hoarding and altering her Xanax prescription, changing the number of pills from 10 to a 90. He said they had now stopped the drugs and were getting help. I didn't really believe it. I agreed to return the children, but I told him I was going to call DSS in Rock Hill and ask them to intervene to protect the kids. Chris got angry; frightened at the possibility that DSS would take the children regardless of what he and Lisa did. After we hung up I called DSS.

Immediately after Thanksgiving DSS conducted their investigation. Because of the history of domestic violence, they wouldn't leave the children in the home unless a third party lived there to insure the children's safety. Chris and Lisa had no choice. Their friend David moved in with them. But David couldn't be there all the time, and one day in early January of 2006, while he was gone, DSS came to check. Finding no third party, they told Lisa they had to take the children and sent the police to get them. Lisa panicked. She grabbed the children and ran, terrified she would lose them. She didn't know what to do. She drove around Rock Hill for several hours trying to decide. Eventually she came to grips and returned. DSS gave Chris and Lisa twenty-four hours to find an acceptable Family Alternative Placement to foster care. If not, they would take the children the following day.

An hour later we got the call from DSS in Rock Hill, a call we had been expecting. They asked if we would consider being the Alternative Family Placement rather than see the children go to foster care. If so, we had until the following day to come and get them. If we didn't take them, they would be placed in foster care, and there was no guarantee they would be placed together.

From stories I had heard about foster care and from my own experience as a Guardian ad Litem, I pictured my grandchildren abandoned, torn from their mother and father, torn from each other. They would be raised like cattle by uneducated people, spending their lives watching endless, mindless TV, eating garbage food, becoming mindless, uneducated failures. Right or wrong, that was my belief—more or less.

We didn't want to become 60-something parents. But this was "it!" This would be for the rest of our lives. I wanted my freedom. I wanted to travel and see the rest of the world and spend time with my friends and still be romantic with my beautiful wife. But I think we always knew this awaited us.

We drove to Rock Hill early the next day and met with the DSS caseworker. We signed some papers, asked a few questions and then drove to the "little house of horrors" to pick up the children. My conversation with the parents was brief, stilted. I was angry. Unbelievably, they were angry too. They seemed to blame us for their situation—as if everything would have been all right if we hadn't butted in and called DSS—as if there would have been no more violence, no more drug use in their lives.

Once again we packed the children into the car and left for home. By this time, for Christopher, going home with Grammy and BC was just a normal part of life. Bree was still just a baby. We would do our best to be good surrogate parents and minimize the trauma of the circumstances in the coming years.

We arrived home late, tired, depressed, worried and reluctantly resigned to an unknown future.

After getting them settled we went to bed wondering. I drifted off looking into my crystal kaleidoscope: PTAs and diapers, trying to relate to parents young enough to be my children, losing our old friends, our freedom.

But we had no choice. This was the right thing to do, at whatever cost to our cushy retirement life as we had loved it.

Chapter 58.
Maybe Just A Bad Dream

I awoke the next morning thinking it was all a bad dream.

*What the hell—? What is this! What's that annoying sound? Must be a bad dream. I see my cat, all orange and cute just sitting there in the middle of the floor, staring. But **what is** that annoying sound?*

"Grammmmmyyyyyy! "Grammmmyyyyyy"

What the hell-? Why am I so annoyed? Angry! Tired! What's going on here? Is this some stupid joke? Why do I feel like crying? I'm so tired!...Oh, I remember, they're our responsibility now. I'm feeling a little worn down. But they need us. I want my life back. I want to be with adults my age, not people half my age who look at me as if to say, "What are you doing here, Old Man?" "Are you lost, Old Man?"

Why, yes—yes I am.

There it is again! "Grammmmmy, Grammmmmmy!"

Now, I know these reflections sound cowardly and melodramatic. I know that Les and I are fortunate to have so much and that, relatively speaking, any hardships imposed on us by these children have been a matter of choice. And

I know the world is crammed full of people in such desperation as to make ours look trivial.

But at that moment, when our life was being turned upside down, I wasn't thinking about the relative nature of our pain. I don't think people do that. A guy who grabs a red-hot poker doesn't muse, *Gee, I wonder if this hurts as much as a bolt of lightening.* He just wants to drop the poker and get rid of the pain. And if he curses and swears and screams and hollers, he's just trying to cope with his pain at that moment. Maybe later, when the pain subsides enough he might think, *Sure did hurt! But probably not as much as when my friend Ralph fell into the wood chipper.*

Maybe, relatively speaking, a red-hot poker is easier than long term, sustained discomfort. That's over and done. I'm not so sure about the wood chipper.

But even long-term discomfort is relative, and after feeling sorry myself, I kicked myself in the pants and took a moment to look around at what so many others have to live with. I realized that the worst I could really say about these kids was that they were an unplanned inconvenience.

In time the shock wore off, we settled into a routine and we find reward in their unquestioning trust, endearing naiveté, hugs and cuddles and laughs at their guileless kids' comments. "BC, you're really old. You're going to die soon aren't you?"

"How long do you think I have, Bree? A few years?"

"Oh, BC, not that long."

I see things I would never have if not for my grandson—things old people don't look for: deer in the deep

It'll Be Okay In The Morning

woods at night, their eyes reflecting the light from my MOPED as we scoot along, a red hawk sitting in the middle of the road feasting on a squirrel as we fly by inches from his blacktop dining table, thousands of tiny, little fingernail-sized baby frogs scurrying across the road before sun up escaping into the woods before birds can gobble them up, orange-stripped baby alligators hiding among the lagoon reeds with their mom looking on. "You stay away from my babies.!" A satellite skimming across the night sky, a once-in-a-lifetime remarkable eclipse of the moon and so much more.

During this first sabbatical for the kids the parents entered into an agreement with DSS. If they successfully completed a program of rehabilitation, they would get their children back. The provisions of the agreement were boilerplate activities doled out by DSS like placebos in an effort to change sick, bad people into good parents: in-patient treatment, subsequent out-patient care, join AA, take a parenting class, drug testing, etc. The program was, as are all government programs, well intentioned. But the formula and follow up were incredibly naive and assumed the people receiving the help wanted it and could sustain new, improved, enlightened behavior after the support rugs had been pulled out.

As a first step, Chris and Lisa returned to an in-patient rehabilitation program. Chris completed his, but Lisa was asked to leave for rules infractions. They decided to move to Hilton Head to be close to the kids.

After six months, Lisa's failure notwithstanding, DSS returned the children. We gave them up with mixed feelings. We had invested a lot of ourselves, given up a lot. And while we got our freedom back, we regretted the children going backwards, worried that the progress we helped them make might be wasted. We hoped for the best. And things got off to a good start. We began to enjoy a peaceful interlude, lulled into a false sense of safety.

Lisa found a job, and Chris began living a dream, playing music with his good friend Eddy. They had a regular schedule of gigs around the Island. I was proud of my son, wary of my daughter-in-law, but lulled. I wanted to think the nightmare had ended. But shame on me! I knew better.

We wanted to help.

Chapter 59.
The House That 'Crack" Built 2006—2007

Chris and Lisa and the kids moved into a four-bedroom town home we bought on the assumption that we could be "kinder-gentler" landlords if they fell on hard times. Les modified the fourth bedroom, downstairs behind the garage, into a separate efficiency for them to rent and help them with expenses.

Things were going so well that I tumbled into a state of foolish euphoria. We were free again! And toward the end of 2006 I began planning another trip to Italy. We promised we would go back after spending a month touring the country several years before: the Dolomites, the Adriatic Coast, The Apennines. We saw Sorrento and stayed in a lovely villa in Positano overlooking the Mediterranean. I fell in love with Italy and wanted to go on another adventure with Les to try and find my 'Cosacchi roots'. So, this time we were going to Calabria and Sicily and explore the small towns in the mountains and along the Adriatic coast. I re-learned a lot of Italian, knowing people in those little towns were unlikely to speak English. We were both excited. By September of 2007 we were ready for our historic, exciting October Italian adventure.

Early in October, a few weeks before we were to leave, Chris and Lisa splurged and went to a rock concert in Jacksonville. When they returned, we noticed red marks on Chris' face. We asked what happened, and he told us that Lisa hit him. He passed over it lightly as if he had been stung by a bee or bumped into a wall. "Oh, it's been going on for a while now, off and on. You know Lisa." I nodded as though I really did know Lisa—as though I really understood, but I was telling myself, *Here we go again.*

It took just a couple of days for the inevitable call to come. "Dad, Lisa's lost it! She's out of control. She's threatening and abusive at night. She's screaming and hollering at me in front of the kids. She saw me walking Christopher home from the bus stop today, lowered the car window and yelled, "Hey, asshole!" loud enough for the general population to hear. I can't be around her, Dad, and I'm afraid to leave the kids with her."

I thought, *Oh, no! Bye-bye Italy!*

I said, "So, what are you going to do?"

"I don't know, Dad, when she gets this way—like she is now—I go downstairs until she cools down, but she has the kids jump off the couch up there to make noise and get me to come out. She's doing it now…listen."

He lifted the phone from his ear and held it up to the ceiling, and we heard the intermittent "thump, thump" as the children performed for their mother, trying to force Dad out of his fall-out shelter.

I thought, *Why is he calling me? What could we do? God I hope he doesn't want to move in with us with the kids! God Damn Lisa.*

He continued, "I'm afraid to be in the same room with her—afraid she'll get violent. And if she does and I call the

Police, it will be my word against hers, and they might arrest me. They've done it before."

My shoulders slumped. My chin dropped to my chest. My head swung back and forth like an elephant's trunk. I spewed a litany of vulgarities like a sacrilegious rosary, "S—t, f—k, God damn son of a bitch!"

The dream trip to Italy was cancelled.

In an effort to try and help, we offered to spend nights there and sleep over to keep the peace until something else could be worked out.

We took turns for a few nights. But we didn't sleep. Lisa was gone when we got there—out on the town. She came back late at night swirling up the stairs like a dust devil smirking, laughing, taunting, insulting, threatening,

"OOOh, mama's boy needs his daddy and mommy to protect him from mean old Lisa. YOU'RE A LOSER! You hear me, A LOSER! Your father is a loser. Your whole family is just a bunch of losers. I don't need you. I don't want you in my life. You're a bum. Get out of my life."

We were too frightened to confront her. We didn't know what she was going to do. We hoped the children sleeping above on the third floor wouldn't wake and hear. She left again and didn't come back for several hours, quietly this time.

We survived a few nights. But we couldn't be there to maintain a truce all the time. And Chris finally called the police when Lisa physically attacked him again and again. It took the police three trips to believe him. Finally, on the third visit, the smashed chair Lisa had put her knee through and Chris' black eye convinced them. They arrested her.

Chris had already decided to separate again. He got help from CODA, a non-profit organization dedicated to supporting victims of domestic violence.

The day of the hearing I drove Chris the 35 miles to Beaufort. He didn't want me to appear with him. He still had some pride. He wanted to do this himself. I waited in the car and caught a glimpse of Lisa walking toward the courthouse with someone I presumed was her attorney. I had a serious uh-oh premonition.

After an hour Chris returned. He tried to look calm, but his jawbone was visibly pulsing as he ground his teeth and his nostrils kept flaring. Things hadn't gone well. The judge not only found against *him* but also gave Lisa the town home. Judge Fender told him to get out, and gave Lisa custody of the children.

I had been to family court several times as a Guardian ad Litem. I had seen judges make off-the-wall decisions, shooting craps with people's lives, imposing personal bias in social experiments without having to bear responsibility for their wrong-headed decisions. But this was the most outrageous.

We rushed back to Hilton Head, retained a competent attorney and immediately filed and obtained a reversal through some sane Judge. Although Chris only received shared custody of the children, he retained the town home. Lisa moved out. But once again Chris and Lisa didn't really separate. The time and money spent on the attorney was wasted. They continued frequent conjugal visits in the town home.

Another bad dream ended, but the coming year, 2008, would bring back the couple's horrific downward spiral.

Chapter 60.
Searching for Another Bottom

Early in January of 2008 I ran my first and only half marathon. I looked forward to having my son and my grandson there to cheer me across the finish line. But Chris didn't make it. Instead he left a message with Les asking to see me. I stopped by the town home after the race. We sat at the kitchen table. He smiled at me coyly, "Is there anything you want to tell me Dad?" I said, "No, except I missed you today. Sorry you couldn't make it." He continued, "You mean you didn't report me?"

'Report you for what?"

"Come on, Dad who told you?"

"Chris, I don't know what you're talking about."

"You mean you didn't tell DSS I was using drugs?"

"No, Chris. Have you been using?"

I tried to sound objective, detached, and rational. But I was his dad, and I had seen this before. Outside I was calm, but my insides were tumbling about. *I wonder what's going on inside him right now. He looks too calm. Didn't he learn anything the first or second or third or fourth or umpteenth time he relapsed?*

But Chris was blasé. "It's no big deal, Dad; it was just a one-time thing. Everyone relapses occasionally. I'm okay now."

I wasn't convinced.

A few weeks went by before we received the call we expected. But I didn't anticipate the panic.

"Dad, please come." Chris was crying. "Dad, help me. I almost died last night. I'm sorry. Please help me. Please come."

This was my son, or what was left of him. Part of me wanted to hold him and tell him it would be all right as though he was still a little boy. But he wasn't a little boy, and another part of me was very frightened and angry.

When I arrived at the town-home, Lisa was pulling out of the driveway. She saw us but didn't acknowledge us. She appeared to be angry and in a hurry. I rang the bell and stepped inside. "Hello. Hello, Chris." He appeared at the top of the steep, narrow staircase, a silhouette against the light from behind. He came plodding down the stairs, shirtless, crying. "Dad, Dad, I'm sorry. Dad, hold me, please hold me." He reached down, took my arms and tried to pull them around him in an embrace. My arms fell back against my sides. I wanted to hold him but told myself, *I can't. He has to do this himself. He has to live it alone.*

I told him he had to call DSS immediately, and if he didn't, we would. I left him standing alone in the narrow entry.

Chris called DSS. Both Chris and Lisa signed the children over to us again as temporary custodians. Chris entered another in-patient program in Georgia. Lisa didn't admit that she was using drugs but didn't object to our taking the children.

When Chris returned from the thirty-day program, he had all the right words. He tried to mend fences with all people he had let down, and he promised to break off from Lisa. But he couldn't. She pursued him relentlessly, calling him twenty or thirty times every day, trying to flush him out.

She succeeded, and then another bottom waited.

Sometime before this, in December 2007, Chris found another boarder for the downstairs bedroom in the townhouse—a good person. He had a responsible job and always paid his rent. He called me one day and asked to meet me. When we met, he begged me to let him out of his lease. He cried and told me he couldn't live there anymore. He was afraid the police would come because of all the drugs Chris and Lisa were using, and he didn't want to be involved. He told me Lisa had been coming downstairs banging on his door at two and three o'clock in the morning begging for money for crack. He said he gave her money because she wouldn't stop the banging until he did. And he was terrified that if he didn't, she would implicate him. He begged me to let him leave and break his lease.

He was gone the next day, leaving Chris without the renter, no work nor any prospects, having burned all his bridges again. He sold or hocked everything he owned, his drums, Klipsch Speakers and all his professional sound equipment worth thousands of dollars.

Lisa contributed to the fiasco, lying and begging a friend for bail money, telling her she had to get Chris out of jail. The two of them attempted to steal a case of Scotch from Reilly's Liquor store but were caught and ran. They escaped but were identified, and a warrant was issued for their arrest. In just three days they wasted more than $8,000 on crack cocaine.

Chris no longer had any sense of reality, still protesting that he was okay—thinking he would get it back together any day now. He hadn't paid any rent in two months. We couldn't rent the now-vacant fourth bedroom, knowing Chris and Lisa were upstairs doing crack. With great difficulty I forced him out of the town home. "I'm not leaving, Dad, I'll pay the rent—your damned blood money rent. I'll get the money. I'll be fine. I just need a little time. Dad, I've got no place to go. I'm not going."

After begging and pleading with him, he finally moved out and moved in with Lisa.

They went into debt with one of the drug dealers. He took their car for non-payment and returned it a couple of days later peppered with bullet holes. But Lisa was undeterred. She tried to pay for their next supply of crack with a wad of plain paper wrapped up in a ten-dollar bill. It didn't work. The dealer pressed a gun to her temple threatening to blow her head off. They gave him something—anything of value.

They settled to the bottom. Conscience numbed, replaced by rationalizations; "It's not my fault…If they hadn't…If I just could have…" Again Chris caught hold of himself long enough to get help. He checked into Any Lengths Rehab facility in Sumter, South Carolina.

Lisa couldn't get into a program as quickly. Rather than see her wind up dead from an overdose or shot to death by a drug dealer, her mother, Pat Pierotti, flew in from Las Vegas to try and protect her. Pat saved Lisa from the predators who came knocking on the door late at night like ghouls to pick over remains of the almost-dead.

During her two-week vigil Pat diligently sat in the living room each night after Lisa went to bed, a sentinel against the threats of irate drug dealers, placing her own safety at risk. She never knew Lisa climbed out her bedroom window each night prowling for crack, returning before sunrise like a damned wandering soul.

Lisa entered rehab about two weeks after Chris in late July 2008 at The Owl's Nest in Florence, South Carolina. Once again she lasted only a few weeks until mid-September when she was kicked out for disobeying the rules and antagonizing the staff and other patients. She called Chris. He still had months to go at Any Lengths. But she convinced him that he had had enough rehabilitation. They moved to Charleston, first living in a little place on Folly Beach and then separately in nearby single-sex halfway houses while they continued their rebound.

Chapter 61.
We Needed An Attorney

We abided and adjusted to our new old life with children, resigned to the likelihood of having them for the duration—our duration. Still, we had only temporary custody pending their parents' successful completion of the second DSS checklist. We were not concerned about the children being returned in the foreseeable future.

- Neither parent had done what was proscribed. Both were in contempt of the court order of February 2008 to refrain from drugs.
- Neither had completed the required in-patient program.
- Both were still wanted on Hilton Head for the attempted robbery.
- Lisa had not completed the Anger Management Program imposed on her by the court after punching Chris in the eye.

We were wary but unconcerned when we had to return to court for a six month DSS review in January 2009. We didn't think we needed an attorney.

But a few days before the review we found out that Chris was asking for unsupervised visitation privileges in Charleston. We, along with the DSS caseworker, disagreed.

Charleston was 100 miles away. We couldn't supervise visitation there and had no idea who would or what would happen to the children in Charleston. We believed it would be dangerous.

The morning of the review the yawning open foyer of the old courthouse was teeming with plaintiffs and defendants and DSS case workers and an army of attorneys representing everyone—except us.

We passed through security and seated ourselves on one of the long, hard wooden benches, the stain and varnish polished to a lustrous patina from the rubbings of thousands of good and bad butts.

Chris arrived with his court-appointed attorney, a gruff-looking bulldog dog of a man. Grady Brown looked loaded for bear as he approached the DSS attorney, Tracy Klatt. A conversation ensued between the two about the visitation request, and I listened and watched as the DSS attorney wilted. They ended their conversation, and Tracy approached our DSS Case Worker, Teresa Parker.

They were out of earshot, but I knew I was being left out of important negotiations that directly impacted the children and us. I drew closer trying to hear Tracy. "But he wants to see his children, and if he can arrange transportation, why not?" Tracy posed to Teresa—more a statement than a question. Teresa looked confused. "Well, I don't know. It's such a long way and…" I stepped into the conversation, "What's going on?" Tracy all but ignored me as if I had no business sticking my nose in.

Teresa summarized, "Tracy thinks Chris should have visitation with the children in Charleston if he can arrange transportation."

"I thought we all agreed. That will not work." I said. "It would be four hours round trip plus two more for Chris just to get here. The kids would spend most of their time in a car. We would have no idea what the children were doing—who would be supervising the visitation. And there should be no unsupervised visitation with their mother. She is also in Charleston, and we have no way of knowing—nor do we trust Chris at this point to honor that prohibition. We all agreed this would not be a good thing."

Grady Brown, Chris' bulldog attorney, shuffled over and escorted Tracy away. They tried to sequester themselves in an anteroom. I shoved my foot and shoulder in the doorway trying to prevent DSS from caving to Chris and his attorney, wondering where our agreement had gone.

Grady glowered, "If you don't get out, I'll call a deputy." I pulled away. They pushed the door closed.

When they reappeared, I knew they had come to an agreement that did not include our wishes and concerns. I turned to Teresa. She looked bewildered. She muttered, "What's going on?" What's happening?"

Les and I were worried and frustrated. How could we stop this? Les wondered, "What are we going to do?"

I whined, "I should have called an attorney. I should have called Nick Felix. The Guardian's Office said he was the best. I should have called."

Nick Felix was an attorney from Hilton Head. His daughters swam on the swim team with our grandson, Christopher. We had a passing relationship and chatted occasionally. He knew our situation.

We waited for our case to be called. I didn't know if we would even be granted the chance to address the court. I leaned my head back, my eyes settled on the top of the formal, long, broad staircase that ran up the center of the hall to the second floor. And there, standing at the top chatting, was Nick Felix. He descended the staircase. All that was missing from this scene was the cloud and the halo. He stopped at the bottom, recognized me and walked over. "Hey Brian, how are you doing?"

Nick's case that morning had been continued. He had time. He listened and went to court with us that morning. Tracy Klatt backed off her accommodation to Chris. Grady Brown argued to the brink of contempt. But Nick prevailed. We sighed. Once again, it seemed, in our desperation, God had plunked someone down in our path. We left court relieved but knew there would be a next round in three months. The parents could ask for the children back if they completed the check list and cleared up the outstanding warrants. We asked Nick to represent us. We wouldn't take anything for granted next time.

A month later the couple moved back to Hilton Head, still officially separated but still living together. Chris made another effort to break away from Lisa or at least to avoid further violent episodes by finding a roommate and moving out. They still kept company and continued their recovery and wanted to get their kids back.

They continued to blame us for their problems. Occasionally Pat and Mike Pierotti called to talk to the kids, and in our brief conversations they blamed Chris for all of Lisa's woes, "It's his responsibility. She's his wife. He just can't leave her alone. He pushes her buttons."

It'll Be Okay In The Morning

It was true. It appeared impossible for Chris to pull away from Lisa. But neither of Lisa's parents would acknowledge Lisa's psychological problems—her borderline personality/bi-polar illness that seemed to make her so much more vulnerable to drug abuse. They didn't want to know. It was easier to blame others for her failings—and for theirs.

The months passed without incident. A "final, final" DSS court date was set ironically for Saint Patrick's Day, March 17, 2009.

We gave Nick all the information we had so he could build our case. The file was more than three inches thick; ten years of Greek Tragedy drug use and violence repeated over and over. We met with Nick and discussed our position. Under no circumstances should the parents regain custody of the children at this time, nor for several years to come—perhaps never. They had wasted opportunity after opportunity to straighten themselves out. Their history of drug abuse, violence and petty crime extended for more than a decade.

Another half inch was added to the file when we discovered Lisa had totaled their car the previous October (2008) after leaving The Owl's Nest. (She had totaled another car in spring of 2006, crashing into a tree on Hilton Head and flipping it over onto its top. She escaped both accidents without injury.) After the October 2008 accident her license was suspended for driving without insurance. But she purchased another *clunker* in January 2009 while living in Charleston. She was subsequently stopped twice more for traffic violations. Her license was revoked and she was required to appear in Charleston court in February.

Even without these recent transgressions, the file was so bloated with misconduct that we knew they wouldn't get their children back on March 17. They were struggling to survive. We believed it would take years of responsible living—at least three or four—before reunification could be considered. And we believed it would be difficult at best. Maybe Chris had a chance, but he would have to leave Lisa for good.

DSS was anxious to close this albatross of a case. It was the second time around for a case lasting more than three years—an eternity on the DSS clock. This court date would be more about the give and take of the conditions under which the parents could be part of Christopher and Bree's lives.

March 17 arrived. The courthouse was filled with its usual herd of attorneys. They began their "lawyers quadrille:" swing your partner, skip to my law suit.

Nick arrived. The three of us commandeered a small conference room adjacent to the courtroom. No one else had arrived yet. Nick was adamant, "If they insist on pursuing this, I'll pull out all the stops." We reviewed highlights of the three-inch thick file: 12 police reports of domestic violence, repeated drug use, rehabilitation and relapse, felony conviction, petty crime, and a contempt citation. The conclusion should be obvious to the court. But the DSS attorney and caseworker had been as meek as lambs, and the Court had been reluctant to take action against the parents.

Teresa Parker, the DSS worker, joined us. She had been a friend but overburdened with so many tired, poor and huddled masses yearning. We probably expected too much of her. We all chatted earnestly, shaking our heads and repeating, "Well, we're all on the same page. We'd all like to close this case and leave it up to the parents to petition the court to get their children back." Nick added, "It'll never happen with people like this." I chafed, realizing he was talking about my son. I wouldn't accept that.

Chris' attorney arrived. Then Chris and Lisa with her attorney and finally the DSS attorney. I thought of the thousands, millions of dollars lost defending the rights of these offenders. Then I thought of the thousands we had to spend to save these children. It didn't seem fair. I pushed it down.

Nick excused himself to talk to Chris and his attorney, hoping to miraculously break through to my son. He returned shortly shaking his head. He commented that Lisa was out there too, occasionally interrupting with bursts of, "I'm a good mother! My kids miss me. They cry for me!" In fact, her kids never mentioned her at all. She hardly ever called and rarely saw them.

The old Clerk of the Court tapped on the peek-a-boo window of our little situation room. He opened the door a crack. "Cosacchi." He knows us. We've been here before. It's time.

The entourage of plaintiffs, defendants, DSS workers and attorneys filed into court. Each attorney spoke briefly, anticipating Judge Fuge's next move.

"Look, folks, this case has been going on too long. I expect you all can come to some kind of an agreement that will protect these children while recognizing the rights of these parents. DSS can't baby-sit these people. Can you see what you can come up with if I give you a little time?" No one dared refuse.

The attorneys met and began a tag-team negotiating contest, bouncing back and forth between themselves and their clients. "Well, how 'bout this—or that—I think this will work and gives you yada yada…" We trusted Nick. He did the best he could for us and the children.

Chapter 62.
Continuing Our New Adventure!

The deal was struck! Les and I were given permanent custody of the children and the parents would be entitled to regular visitation as long as they conformed to the requirements of the agreement which were many:
- No domestic violence
- No criminal activity
- No use of illegal drugs
- Provide evidence of drug tests upon request
- Live a life committed to AA/NA
- Receive/continue ongoing counseling and medication
- Provide written confirmation on request
- Lisa receive psychiatric evaluation and treatment
- Provide a very nominal monthly child support payment

A visitation schedule was outlined, and our new life continued. We still had the children. They were safe. But now we had to deal with the parents every week, sometimes two or three times. We wanted to make it work for the children and for ourselves and even for the parents. There was still a flickering ray of hope they might one day be a positive influence on their children. So, while we were not obliged, we initially tried to help by dropping the children off and picking them up when either Chris or Lisa couldn't find transportation. But in time we stopped helping Lisa. We couldn't put up with her irrational attacks—her fusillades of accusations and sarcasm.

On two occasions she refused to return the children at the proper time. And we had to decide whether to call the police and traumatize the children or cave and let her keep them, not knowing when she would return them or what she might do the next time.

On one of those occasions we extended Lisa's visitation so she could join us and attend an art exhibition Christopher had entered at school. During the proceedings Bree told Lisa she was uncomfortable 'down there'..."It hurts when I pee."

We had recently taken Bree to the pediatrician twice for a urinary infection, but Bree had not mentioned it in several days. We assumed it was under control.

Lisa confronted us with the information, irate and accusing, "What's the matter with you people letting MY daughter suffer with some kind of God-knows-what infection?"

Les didn't fight back. Instead she responded calmly, telling Lisa we had been to the doctor with Bree twice and thought the problem was getting better but that we would call immediately and see if we could get Bree to the doctor right away. It was Friday, and we didn't want Bree to have to wait until Monday.

Les left to go to the car to call the doctor on her cell phone. When she left, Lisa stopped her objections and accusations and decided she wasn't going to wait. "Oh, she'll be all right until Monday. It's no big deal." She walked out of the building holding Christopher and Bree by the hands and with me following thinking, *Whoa, what's going on—hold it—stop—wait.* When she got outside with the children, she started to leave while Les was on the phone just ten yards away. Lisa put Bree in the bicycle's "caboose" and started to try and pedal away from the school.

I stood for a moment, debating what to do. *Bree should get to the doctor. Lisa is leaving. If she leaves, Bree will not get to the doctor. She shouldn't do this!*

I tried to stop her.

"Lisa, wait! Les is on the phone with the doctor's office. Let's get Bree to the doctor."

She refused. "No, I'm not waiting!" She pulled away. She told Christopher to get on his bike and Bree to stay in the caboose. It was quite a scene! People were exiting the school, gawking at the escalating spectacle. I tried to restrain her, first holding the bicycle's handle bars. She pushed me away, and I grabbed her arm. I GRABBED HER ARM! When I saw myself, alarms went off, and I let go as if her arm were a hot poker. I pleaded with her, "Lisa, just wait a minute—just a minute! Let's see when we can get Bree into the doctor—just wait." She responded, "I'm not waiting. I'm not going to the doctor. This is my visitation time. We're not going—<u>Not on my time</u>."

Les got off the phone and implored me to let her go. Lisa peddled off with the children: Christopher on his bicycle, Bree screaming in the caboose.

After a brief discussion, Les drove after Lisa, caught up to her and convinced her to let Les take Bree to the doctor, assuring Lisa that Bree could then be returned to Lisa. Bree was fine. Lisa had her last extended visitation. We would go by the book from then on!

Months went by. Les diligently went through the exercise each week of trying to let Chris and Lisa know of the children's activities: school events, teachers' conferences, swim schedule/ meets, Cub Scouts, PTA, soccer, gymnastics, church events and on and on. And every week some new attack, some new complaint from Lisa.

After the first six months the visitation schedule changed, giving the parents more time with the kids, including overnights. It would be complicated. The parents were separated, and decisions had to be made as to who would get the children when. We asked Jan Cook, one of our church pastors, to mediate a meeting with Chris and Lisa to clarify the changes. Jan did her best. For the first five minutes Lisa was quiet, smiling, smirking, smoldering, waiting. When she could no longer hold back, she took the stage, attacking, blaming, accusing, berating, defending, going off on dozens of tangents. Jan tried to calm her, but Lisa was uncontrollable and walked out of the meeting. Then she walked back in—then out—then in—then out, her long wispy tresses and all her demons trailing behind her. We drew our conclusions without her but made sure her new visitation rights were respected.

Chris seemed to be making progress. He was attending regular AA meetings. He got a job as a waiter. And despite complaints about one thing or another he stuck with it.

For the next year we lived on the hope that Chris would continue his recovery. And we knew, as did all his friends in AA, that if he were to survive, it would be without Lisa. We didn't hold out hope for her.

Chapter 63.
Lisa's Final Collapse—For Now

In March 2010, almost two years after the court agreement, we began to get warning signs. Something was happening to Lisa. She was even less predictable, always agitated. Chris warned us—told us she was using again. We had no proof. We weren't sure. She didn't seem to be posing any threat to the children on visitations. I didn't want to waste money on a drug test knowing Lisa was creatively conniving. (In 2005, she had her five-year-old son pee into the drug test specimen cup for her.)

But Chris was sure she was using. He would get the proof.

In early April 2010 he visited Lisa in her apartment. He played along, "the spider and the fly." She offered to go out and buy some crack for the two of them. When she returned, crack in hand, it was all the proof he needed. He ran from the apartment. He called us and recounted the story. We understood the risk he had taken.

We decided to stop visitation immediately. But that decision was unnecessary. Lisa was no longer very interested in her children. Crack had taken over again. A few days later she was evicted from her apartment. She started moving from place to place with virtually nothing but the clothes on her back. She was fired from both her jobs for absenteeism and violent outbursts. I stopped by the Pizza Hut where she had been working for more than a year to see if they had any information. She had been doing well there. I spoke to her supervisor "Lisa? She's gone—doesn't work here anymore. You have her kids? Well, if I were you I wouldn't let her anywhere near them."

Chris' devotion compelled him to try and help her one more time. Through friends in AA, he petitioned Any Lengths, the treatment facility he had last entered in Sumter two years before. He begged them to give her a chance.

They let her in.

But Lisa's illnesses were out of control. She lied and cheated and lasted only seven weeks before they told her to leave. She returned to Hilton Head.

A few weeks later, in early July, she wound up knocking on Chris' door at two o'clock in the morning, high on crack and needing a partner. There was little left of the person he loved. He pleaded with her one last time to get help. But she attacked. "You're a bum. You're no good—a loser. Don't touch me! Get away." He opened the door and reached out to her, "You better go." Lisa screamed at him, "Bastard!" She lashed out, smashing him on the head with her crack pipe. Then she turned and ran into the night.

Chris called the police. They tracked her down and arrested her. Lisa's condition was so severe that Chris had her involuntarily committed. She was taken to the psychiatric ward at Beaufort Hospital and held there in lock-up until a bed was found at a State treatment facility in Charleston. She spent the next three weeks at Palmetto Mental Health until a judge released her.

It'll Be Okay In The Morning

With nothing and no place else to go, she returned to Hilton Head again. Two weeks later she wound up in the emergency room. She had been living with a drug dealer who got too rough. She thought her arm was broken. This time the police tried to help.

Once more Lisa was sent involuntarily to the Beaufort Psych Ward and then on to Morris Village, another State facility in Columbia. After a week she appeared before another judge, who ordered her to remain there for the maximum period of sixty days. But a week later she fled, heading back to Hilton Head, and within three weeks she was finally arrested on major criminal charges.

She had been traveling with an older male companion—a fellow who had, the year before, held her against her will in his home for several days but was now her "crack buddy." He was wanted by the police in two states for a variety of criminal behaviors. When they stopped at a local gas station, the police recognized him. They approached the car. Lisa panicked and fled. She jumped into a car at an adjacent gas pump and threatened the driver and his child. The frightened driver complied, and they drove off. A short time later she jumped from the car and fled. She was apprehended later in a hotel room at the south end of the island with her crack dealer and charged with carjacking, kidnapping and use of a deadly weapon in the commission of a crime. The story and her sad photograph made the headlines in the local paper.

We had to tell the kids for fear they might find out from other children at school. Not an easy thing to do. They received the news the way we expected.

Christopher was stoic, changing the subject immediately, "Hey, look did you see my..." We don't know what goes on inside him. Bree initially seemed to accept it for what it was, "I'm mad at Mom. She shouldn't use those drugs. It's sad." But she woke that night with night terrors, trembling. She nestled in Les' arms, and then peed on the floor.

But the sun rose again. Bree lost a tooth, and the prospect of the tooth fairy making a visit came at the right time.

Lisa remains in jail on $70,000.00 bond. No one, including her parents, was willing to put up the money to get her out. She would be a flight risk and a risk to her own safety.

For now she is safe in prison. We sleep a little easier at night.

Chris filed for divorce and, please God, may have finally pulled away from her. We're proud of him. He has had mountains to climb—so many scars that may never heal.

I spoke to the solicitor who will be prosecuting Lisa's case.

"She is likely to go to jail, but there is no guarantee. There is no minimum sentence for these offenses. She could get up to thirty years just for the kidnapping charge, but she might also be released with 'time served.'

But, then again, who knows what can happen in the next couple of months."

Yes, indeed, who knows?

Chapter 64.
Intermission

The story has slowed for a YIELD sign. Not the end, just a pause—an intermission while we wait for the next exciting episode. Harrison, New York, Cosacchi's Mountain, Boy Scouts and Altar Boys and all the adventures and scary things that I recall are only <u>most</u> of a lifetime. It's been a hell of a ride, filled with drama.

Maybe it's had more than most but surely not as much as so many others. I look around me now, and I see my life before me, and I count my blessings (almost) every day. I've come to realize that very few get out of this life for free. I have so much to be grateful for—so many exciting, happy times. I've done so much of what I selfishly wanted, so many things I never dreamed of as a kid.

Les and I have seen much of the world. I've checked off many to-do's on my Bucket List; motor cycle lessons, hang gliding, white water rafting, hiking to the bottom of the Grand Canyon, sky diving, biking the Assault On Mt. Mitchell, enjoying the company of so many wonderful friends, and just being a clown. And I've lived longer than I thought I would 30 years ago—long enough to see my own children grow to adulthood and, please God, long enough to see my grandchildren to the end of the dock.

And if it were to end today, I'd be at peace believing my son will be courageous and survive and succeed and love his children; my beautiful, talented, brilliant wife will find some rest; all my grandchildren will thrive.

Brian Cosacchi

My spectacular daughter, our family 'glue,' has been keeping us all together. She has her own challenges including a very successful 'cottage' business, TLC by Tara, creating and producing personalized stationery. She watches over the successes of her children for which she should take some credit but does not. She and her husband Steve have enjoyed their loving marriage for more than twenty years. God give her all the happiness she has ever dreamed of.

For now we will continue to adjust to our old-codger, co-parenting role along with Chris, our son. I hope his role will grow as he and his kids grow together.

They are good kids with unique challenges. But despite their family upheaval, both Bree and Christopher are doing well in school and are coping with the fact that their Mom is gone.

They have tenderness at times that is surprising, and it brings us smiles to know they have good hearts. Last night Christopher and I lay in front of the fireplace watching a football game. Bree came downstairs and draped a quilt over us and tucked us in. She does surprising things like that. Tonight, in late January, she's wrapping homemade "after-Christmas" presents for Grammy and me.

Christopher is a joyful combination of little boy and little man. We vie for Alpha male position. He's goofy and serious and still needs me or Grammy to tuck him in at night. He won't go to bed without that soft touch. We're glad to oblige.

And it's good to have my son back. We missed a lot of good times—a lot of good years. I missed him. I wish I could get that time back. But as Chris frequently tells me; "It is what it is." I can't change the past, and I can't waste pre-

It'll Be Okay In The Morning

cious time regretting my mistakes. Life has been good. God has pitched in when the load got a little too heavy.

So, I will continue to fill my days with some music and some exercise, and maybe find some new way to help someone and wait for the kids to come home. And Les will continue to cope, filling up every minute with an unending list of projects that keep our house the home we all enjoy and are proud of. We would all be lost without her. And we will wait and watch and pray and roll with the tide—so many questions still to be resolved before we go.

So, stay tuned. Tomorrow is another day and, if I'm good, and the last one to go to sleep tonight, maybe everything will be okay in the morning.

Made in the USA
Columbia, SC
03 November 2019